Eulogies

When

Long-Term Illness

Takes Our Beloved:

Writing Guidelines, Examples, and

Templates

J Jordan

Notable+

Copyright & Disclaimer

EULOGIES WHEN LONG-TERM ILLNESS TAKES OUR BELOVED: WRITING GUIDELINES, EXAMPLES, AND TEMPLATES

The author, J Jordan, is represented by Notable Plus LLC, Palm Bay, Florida.

Eulogies When Long-Term Illness Takes Our Beloved: Writing Guidelines, Examples, and Templates
Paperback: 182 Pages
Print Quality: Black ink and 55# (90 GSM) cream paper
ISBN-10: 1-960176-15-3
ISBN-13: 978-1-960176-15-8

Contents

Preface

Firstly, please accept my deepest condolences. Losing a loved one is an incredibly challenging experience, and I sincerely pray that you find the strength to endure during this time of immense pain and loss.

The loss of a loved one due to long term illness, either terminal or chronic, can leave us grappling with a profound mix of emotions. In the midst of sorrow, it becomes crucial to remember the joy and celebrate the life they lived. This book aims to provide guidance and solace for those navigating the complexities of mourning an individual who passed away due to illness. By exploring ways to capture their essence, honor their legacy, and embrace joyful remembrance, we can find healing amidst grief and craft a heartfelt eulogy. Additionally, we will delve into the significance of community support, meaningful rituals of remembrance, celebration of life, advocacy and ultimately finding hope as we move forward. Although the pain may seem overwhelming, it is indeed possible to remember the joy amidst sorrow, keeping the spirit of our loved ones alive in our hearts.

When news of the passing of a loved one arrives, and you find yourself overwhelmed with emotions while simultaneously planning the funeral and holding the rest of the family together, writing a eulogy becomes an arduous task. The raw and gut-wrenching thoughts of your loved one being gone make it challenging to create a eulogy that truly honors their memory. Moreover, amidst all the chaos, you must gather the courage to stand before a grieving audience, paying tribute to the deceased and offering words of encouragement to those in mourning. The weight of this responsibility can feel like an additional burden atop the mountain of challenges you already face.

However, it is a task that must be undertaken, and if you are reading this, it means that this great responsibility has been entrusted to you. I have personally experienced the position you find yourself in right now, and I wholeheartedly empathize with your situation. Despite the overwhelming emotions you may be experiencing, I firmly believe that you possess bravery and courage, even if you may not feel it at this moment.

The eulogy is a unique and distinct type of speech that requires a different approach due to the mental and emotional state of the audience. This book is specifically designed to assist you in this particular task. It is not a generic speech writing guide, as that is not what you need at this moment.

My intention is not to delve into the mechanics of speech writing, but rather to provide you with specific wording, examples and templates that you can adapt, replicate and use to craft your tribute or at least inspire and guide your eulogy writing process.

The body of the eulogy contains crucial sections that we have provided for your convenience. These sections can be customized to suit your specific requirements. Within the eulogies presented in this book, you will find introductions, conclusions, and segments dedicated to sharing cherished memories, highlighting the deceased's passions, discussing their influence, and offering words of comfort to those attending the funeral.

Eulogies employ specific language and sections that enable us to effectively convey the sentiments we wish to express. During challenging times, it can be difficult to find the right words and establish a structure that effectively communicates our emotions while paying tribute to someone who held great significance in our lives.

This book primarily serves as a guide to help you navigate the grieving process and provides examples and templates for eulogy writing. You can largely copy, modify, and adapt these resources to suit the eulogy you are preparing. Its purpose is to alleviate some of the difficulties associated with this task during such a challenging time.

While these eulogies can serve as sources of inspiration, it is important to personalize your tribute to reflect the unique life and relationship you shared with your loved one. Use the structure and themes highlighted here as guides, but make sure to incorporate your own memories, anecdotes, and emotions to create a heartfelt eulogy that truly honors your loved one.

About Sections, Fields, FAQ and More

Sections

This book offers a variety of sections that you can customize and incorporate into your eulogy. The language used in these sections is in line with the common expressions found in eulogies. By eliminating the need to fret over the wording or search for the perfect phrases to express your emotions, writing eulogies becomes a less daunting task.

Fields

We have incorporated specific fields, such as [Name], to conveniently accommodate the inclusion of relevant information about the departed individual. These fields greatly assist in tailoring the eulogies to honor your loved one in a personalized manner.

Tips

Italicized tips are a valuable component designed to ignite creativity and motivation within your writing endeavors. These carefully curated suggestions serve as a catalyst for inspiration, encouraging innovative thinking and the exploration of new ideas.

Prompts

These words serve as a compass for your writing endeavors, urging you to include captivating stories, cherished memories, and entertaining anecdotes.

FAQ

Our Frequently Asked Questions (FAQ) section provides comprehensive answers to common inquiries regarding writing eulogies, as well as coping with loss, healing, and moving forward.

Illness FAQ

In order to assist with eulogies that may reference specific illnesses, we have provided a concise overview of these conditions. However, for more detailed information, we recommend consulting reliable online sources or seeking advice from a medical professional. The purpose of this information is solely to equip you with enough knowledge to eloquently speak on behalf of your departed loved one. It is important to note that this is not medical advice and should not be utilized for diagnostic purposes.

Once again, we extend our deepest condolences to you and your loved ones during this time of need. We sincerely pray that you find the strength to carry on.

1. Writing Eulogies When Long-Term Illness Takes Our Beloved

The process of writing a eulogy is never an easy task, especially when it comes to commemorating the lives of loved ones who succumbed to long term illnesses. This deeply personal responsibility requires careful thought, empathy, and compassion. To honor those we have lost, we must craft a heartfelt eulogy that captures their spirit, celebrates their life, and recognizes the unique challenges they faced. In this chapter, we will explore the important elements of writing a eulogy for those who battled terminal and chronic long term illnesses, acknowledging the strength and resilience of our beloved, and being an advocate for their cause.

1.1 Understanding the Purpose of a Eulogy

Before addressing any specific topic, it is essential to grasp the purpose of a eulogy. This speech serves as a tribute, an opportunity to acknowledge the life and legacy of the deceased. For individuals who endured long term illnesses, it becomes even more crucial to focus on their resilience, courage, and the impact they had on others during their journey. Also, this type of eulogy is often used as a platform to bring attention to the illness that took our loved one and advocate for support to reduce or eradicate the illness.

1.2 The Sections of a Eulogy

There are a number of sections that come together to make a memorable eulogy. In the paragraphs below we highlight some of these sections. Pay attention to the purpose of these sections and note how they are adapted in the eulogy examples and templates in the following chapters.

1.3 Reflecting on Their Life

Begin the eulogy by reflecting on the person's life as a whole, highlighting their accomplishments, interests, and unique qualities. Emphasize the aspects of their personality that shone through, despite their illness. Share anecdotes that illustrate their passions, sense of humor, or strength of character, helping the audience remember them beyond their illness.

1.4 Recognizing the Battle and Strength

Acknowledge the challenges faced by the person due to their long term illness. Recall their unwavering strength, resilience, and determination throughout their journey. Highlight their ability to find hope, joy, and purpose even in the face of adversity. Share stories or examples that demonstrate their bravery and ability to inspire others.

1.5 Paying Tribute to their Support System

Terminal and chronic illnesses often require a strong support system. Use this paragraph to appreciate the efforts of family members, friends, caregivers, and medical professionals who stood by their side throughout the journey. Express gratitude for their unwavering support, selflessness, and dedication.

1.6 Acknowledging Their Impact on Others and Advocacy Activities

Discuss the positive impact the person had on others: their family, friends, colleagues, or community. Highlight the love, compassion, and kindness they spread during their lifetime. Discuss whether they took on an advocacy role to bring awareness to their illness or provided support to others facing similar struggles.

1.7 Sharing Memories

Devote a portion of the eulogy to sharing personal memories of the individual. Recall funny, heartwarming, or meaningful moments that showcase their spirit, zest for life, or defining characteristics. These memories offer comfort to those mourning and provide a more intimate connection to the life being celebrated.

1.8 Inspiring Lessons Learned

Reflect on the lessons learned from witnessing the person's journey with a long term illness. Discuss the importance of cherishing life, finding strength in difficult times, and fostering empathy and understanding for others. Share any wisdom they imparted through their experiences, leaving the audience with valuable insights.

1.9 Addressing Grief and Loss

Gently acknowledge the grief and sadness felt by family and friends. Offer words of support and encouragement, reinforcing the importance of coming together during difficult times. Remind those in mourning that it is natural to feel a range of emotions and that a eulogy serves as a reminder of the love and cherished memories shared.

1.10 Closing with Hope and Celebration

Conclude the eulogy by expressing hope for a brighter future, where the person's memory will continue to inspire and their legacy will live on. Acknowledge the profound impact the deceased had on all who knew them and encourage everyone present to cherish their memory.

Writing a eulogy for individuals lost to long term illness is a challenging task that requires intellect, sensitivity, and compassion. By skillfully crafting a speech that reflects on their life as a whole, acknowledges their battles with illness, and celebrates their remarkable qualities and impact on others, we can ensure that their memory is honored and their story is told with empathy and understanding.

2. The Power of Memories: Honoring Someone Lost to Long Term Illness through Words

2.1. Introduction: The Significance of Memories in Honoring Those Lost to Long Term Illness

Grief is a deeply personal and challenging journey, particularly when it comes to the loss of a loved one due to illness. In these heartbreaking moments, memories become powerful tools for honoring and cherishing the lives of those we have lost. Memories hold the essence of individuals, encapsulating their unique personalities, experiences, and impact on our lives. This chapter explores the profound significance of memories in the grieving process, offering insights into how to navigate the complexities of illness, preserve cherished moments, and find solace through the healing power of words. By sharing stories and embracing memories, we can honor the lives of those we have lost and find strength in their lasting legacy.

2.1.1 The Lasting Impact of Illness

Illness can turn our lives upside down in an instant. The shock and grief that comes with losing someone can leave us feeling lost and overwhelmed. Each person's experience is unique, but one thing remains constant: the lasting impact it has on our lives and our memories.

2.1.2 The Role of Memories in the Grieving Process

Memories are powerful, serving as a bridge between the past and the present. When we lose someone to illness, memories become even more significant. They allow us to celebrate and honor the life that was, to cherish the moments we shared, and to keep their spirit alive within us. Memories become our way of coping and healing.

2.2. Understanding The Impact of Illness: Coping with Unexpected Loss

2.2.1 The Shock and Trauma of Long Term Illness

The profound shock and trauma that accompany the experience of long term illness are emotions that can leave us feeling utterly bewildered. Even when we are aware of a loved one's suffering, the unexpected nature of their loss can make it incredibly challenging to process our own emotions, leaving us overwhelmed and uncertain about how to move forward.

The initial shock and trauma that ensue require time and patience to navigate, as we grapple with the harsh reality of our loved one's absence. Accepting the fact that their life was marred by such immense suffering and has now come to a mortal end can be an overwhelming whirlwind of confusing thoughts and emotions. It becomes a daunting task to reconcile the conflicting notions that their pain has finally ceased, yet they are no longer present with us. This amalgamation of emotions presents us with a formidable challenge to confront and manage.

2.2.2 Navigating the Stages of Grief

The stages of grief, including denial, anger, bargaining, depression, and acceptance, are well-known but can feel like a tumultuous roller coaster ride. Navigating through these stages is a personal journey, and it's important to remember that there is no set timeline for grief. Each person will experience it in their own way, and memories play a crucial role in helping us process and navigate these stages.

2.3. The Healing Power of Words: Exploring The Role of Memories in the Grieving Process

2.3.1 Expressing Emotions Through Writing

Writing provides an outlet for our emotions during the grieving process. It allows us to express our deepest sorrows, joys, and love that we still hold for the person we lost. Through words, we can paint a picture of who they were and how they impacted our lives. Writing gives us the space to release our pent-up emotions and find solace in the memories we hold dear.

2.3.2 Connecting with Memories as a Source of Comfort and Healing

Memories have an incredible power to bring comfort and healing during times of grief. They allow us to relive moments of happiness, laughter, and love shared with our loved one. By reconnecting with these memories, we remind ourselves that their presence, though physically gone, continues to live on in our hearts. Memories become a source of solace, reminding us that while they may be absent from our lives, they will never be forgotten.

2.4. Preserving Memories: Strategies for Capturing and Preserving Cherished Moments

2.4.1 The Importance of Documenting Memories

Documenting memories becomes essential in honoring those we've lost to illness. Whether it's through writing, photography, or other forms of creative expression, capturing these cherished moments ensures that they remain alive and tangible. By documenting our memories, we create a lasting tribute to their impact on our lives and provide future generations with a window into the beautiful soul we were fortunate to know.

2.4.2 Utilizing Different Mediums to Preserve Memories

In this digital age, we have numerous mediums at our disposal to preserve memories. From creating a scrapbook or a memory box filled with mementos to creating online photo albums or dedicating a blog or social media page to our loved one's memory, the possibilities are endless. By utilizing these different mediums, we can ensure that the memories we hold dear are preserved in a way that feels personal and meaningful to us.

Remember, honoring someone lost to illness through words is a testament to their impact on our lives. It allows us to find comfort, healing, and a sense of connection even in their physical absence. The power of memories is immeasurable; they remind us that love transcends time and that the ones we hold dear will forever remain a part of us.

2.5. Crafting a Tribute: Writing Heartfelt Words to Honor the Memory of a Loved One

Losing a loved one to illness is an indescribable pain that leaves a void in our lives. One way to honor their memory is by crafting a heartfelt tribute that captures the essence of their life and the impact they had on those around them. While writing about someone you've lost can be challenging, it can also be a cathartic and healing process.

2.5.1 Reflecting on the Impact of the Lost Loved One

Before you begin writing, take some time to reflect on the impact your loved one had on your life and the lives of others. Think about their unique qualities, their passions, and the memories you shared together. Remember the moments that made you smile, the lessons they taught you, and the ways in which they touched the hearts of those around them.

2.5.2 Tips for Writing a Meaningful Tribute

- Be authentic: Write from the heart and don't worry about being overly formal or eloquent. The most meaningful tributes are those that are genuine and heartfelt.

- Share anecdotes: Highlight specific moments or stories that encapsulate the essence of your loved one. These personal anecdotes can bring their spirit to life and create a deeper connection with readers.

- Focus on their positive qualities: While it's important to acknowledge the pain of loss, also highlight the positive qualities, achievements, and the love they brought into the world. This can become a source of comfort and inspiration for others.

- Use humor if appropriate: Remember that life isn't always serious, and adding a touch of humor can reflect the personality of your loved one and bring warmth to the tribute.

- Edit and revise: After drafting your tribute, give it some time and then come back to it with fresh eyes. Edit and revise as needed to ensure you've captured the essence of your loved one.

2.6. Sharing Memories: Creating a Supportive Community Within the Grieving Process

Grief can often feel isolating, but sharing memories of our loved ones can create a supportive community that understands and empathizes with our pain. Creating a space where people can come together to share stories and memories can be incredibly healing.

2.6.1 Establishing a Safe Space to Share Memories

Whether it's through a private online platform, a memorial event, or a simple gathering with close friends and family, establishing a safe space to share memories can be cathartic. Encourage others to participate by sharing their own stories and experiences, creating a supportive environment where people feel comfortable expressing their grief.

2.6.2 The Importance of Empathy and Active Listening

In these shared spaces, it's crucial to practice empathy and active listening. Everyone grieves differently, and it's important to validate and respect each individual's experience. Focus on being present, offering understanding and support to those who choose to open up. Sometimes, the simple act of listening can provide immense comfort to someone in the midst of their grief.

2.7. Finding Solace Through Storytelling: The Therapeutic Benefits of Sharing Personal Experiences

Sharing personal stories and experiences not only creates a supportive community but also offers therapeutic benefits for both the storyteller and the listener. By sharing our own journeys, we can find solace and help others going through similar experiences.

2.7.1 Healing Through Narrative

Storytelling allows us to process our emotions, unravel our thoughts, and find meaning in the face of loss. As we recount our memories and experiences, we begin to understand ourselves and our grief on a deeper level. Through narrative, we can find healing and make sense of the complex emotions that come with losing someone.

2.7.2 Encouraging Others to Share Their Own Stories

Encouraging others to share their own stories not only provides them with an outlet, but it also allows for a deeper connection within the grieving community. By fostering an environment that encourages storytelling, we create a space where individuals can find support, strength, and understanding in their shared experiences.

2.8. Moving Forward: Embracing Memories as a Source of Strength and Inspiration

While the pain of losing someone never completely fades, embracing memories can help us find strength and inspiration as we navigate life without our loved ones.

2.8.1 Transforming Grief into Resilience

Memories have the power to transform grief into resilience. By reminiscing about the love, joy, and lessons our loved ones brought into our lives, we can draw strength during difficult times. Embracing their memory allows their spirit to live on within us, providing us with the resilience needed to face the challenges that lie ahead.

2.8.2 The Legacy of Memories in Shaping the Future

The memories we hold dear become a unique legacy that shapes not only our individual lives but also the lives of those around us. By cherishing the memories of our lost loved ones, we can keep their legacies alive and carry their influence into the future. Our memories become a guiding light, inspiring us to live fully and embrace the precious moments life has to offer.

As we navigate the painful journey of grieving a loved one lost to illness, we must remember that memories can serve as a source of solace, healing, and inspiration. By capturing and preserving cherished moments, crafting heartfelt tributes, and sharing our stories, we create a supportive community that honors the lives of those we have lost. In embracing memories, we find the strength to move forward, transforming grief into resilience. Let us hold onto the power of memories, allowing them to guide us as we navigate the path of healing and keep the spirit of our loved ones alive.

3. Eulogy Templates and Sections

In the upcoming chapters, we present a collection of eulogies that have been carefully divided into specific sections, each contributing to the creation of a well-crafted eulogy. You are given the freedom to include any or all of these sections, depending on your personal preferences and the circumstances surrounding your situation. Feel empowered to edit and adapt these templates as you see fit, incorporating your own experiences, stories, and quotes into the appropriate sections.

We have curated a collection of eulogies that encompass both generic conditions and specific illnesses, including Heart Disease, Multiple Sclerosis, Cancer, HIV/AIDS, and more. By exploring these examples, you can draw inspiration from their wording, structure, valuable tips and prompts to create a truly memorable tribute for your beloved.

Moreover, our eulogy examples are thoughtfully tailored to various relationships, such as mother, father, brother, daughter, aunt, uncle, and others. This ensures that you can grasp both the similarities and differences when addressing the loss of individuals who held significant meaning in your life.

As you proceed, take note of the themes of advocacy, strength in difficulty and resilience of a life lived with long term illness. The recurring theme of advocacy is common among these eulogies and may be one of the main reasons that you may choose this type of tribute for your loved one.

Crafting a heartfelt eulogy is a delicate task, and we understand the importance of honoring your loved one with utmost respect and professionalism. Our comprehensive collection aims to guide you through this challenging process, providing you with the necessary tools to express your deepest emotions and pay tribute to their remarkable life.

Moreover, you have the option to interchange sections from the different eulogies, allowing you to create a truly unique template. Alternatively, you can use these templates as a source of inspiration to craft your own distinctive eulogy. Our intention is to provide you with valuable assistance during this challenging time. May you find solace and strength to endure this period of loss.

4. Eulogy 1 - In Loving Memory of My Mother: Celebrating Her Strength in the Face of Long Term Illness

4.1 Introduction: Remembering a Remarkable Woman

4.1.1 Remembering a Remarkable Woman

In the depths of our hearts, there are some individuals who leave an indelible mark on our lives. They possess a strength and resilience that inspire us, even in the face of adversity. I am [Your Name], [Name]'s [Your relationship to the deceased] and I am honored to speak on behalf of the loved ones gathered here today to pay tribute. This eulogy is a tribute to the memory of my mother [Name], a remarkable woman who displayed unwavering courage throughout her battle with illness. Through her journey, she taught us invaluable lessons about love, determination, and the beauty of life. Join me as we reflect upon the extraordinary strength [Name] exhibited and celebrate the legacy she left behind.

4.1.2 Reflecting on a Life Well-lived

In this eulogy, we pay tribute to a truly remarkable woman - my mother [Name]. She was a force of nature, always radiating strength and resilience, even in the face of adversity. Her journey through illness showcased her unwavering spirit and served as a source of inspiration to all who knew her. As we reflect on her life well-lived, we celebrate her unyielding determination in the face of challenges and honor the legacy she left behind.

4.1.3 The Loved Ones who Continue [His/Her] Legacy

Our beloved [Name]'s passing has left a profound void in our lives. In reflecting on her life, it is important to acknowledge those who continue to carry her legacy forward. [Name] is survived by [State and name the close kins e.g. her loving family, including her devoted husband, [Name] and their [number] children [List Names], who were the center of her universe.] [State and name other relatives e.g. She leaves behind a host of cherished relatives, including nieces, nephews, and cousins whom she held dear.] Additionally, she touched the lives of countless friends and acquaintances through her graciousness and unwavering support.

Her presence will be greatly missed by all who had the privilege of knowing her. Although this loss brings immeasurable grief, we find solace in knowing that [Name] has engendered a lasting impact on those whose lives she gracefully enhanced with love and joy.

4.2. The Journey Begins: Understanding the Diagnosis

When my mother first received her diagnosis, our world was turned upside down. The initial shock and emotional turmoil were overwhelming, but we knew we had to gather ourselves and face the unknown head-on. We embarked on a journey of understanding, researching every aspect of her illness, and seeking out the best medical advice available. Alongside the medical support, we leaned on our friends and family for emotional support, finding solace in their presence during this trying time.

4.3. A Tale of Courage: Navigating the Challenges of Illness

Facing the challenges of illness requires a tremendous amount of courage, and my mother exemplified this in every step of her journey. As her physical limitations began to manifest, she faced them head-on, adapting her lifestyle and finding new ways to embrace life's joys. Despite the hardships, she maintained an unwavering spirit, never allowing her illness to define her. [Name]'s mental and emotional resilience were truly awe-inspiring, serving as a reminder that the strength within us can triumph over any obstacle.

4.4. A Warrior's Spirit: Celebrating Strength and Resilience

In the face of illness, my mother's warrior spirit shone through. With a contagious positivity and an indomitable determination, she faced each day with grace and gratitude. [Name]'s ability to find joy in the smallest of moments and to cherish the time she had remaining left a lasting impact on everyone around her. Her journey has become a beacon of hope, inspiring others to embrace their own strength and resilience in the face of life's challenges. Though she may be gone, her legacy of unwavering strength lives on, reminding us all to celebrate the power of the human spirit.

4.5. Finding Joy Amidst Adversity: Cherishing Precious Moments

4.5.1 Making the Most of Quality Time and Creating Lasting Memories

Tip: When faced with the challenge of a loved one's illness, it becomes even more important to savor every moment and make the most of the time we have together. Despite the difficulties, finding joy amidst adversity is possible. It's about treasuring the quality time spent with our loved ones and creating lasting memories that will stay with us forever.

Whether it's going on a picturesque hike, cooking a favorite family recipe, or simply sharing laughter over a board game, these moments of connection are what truly matter. By prioritizing these experiences, we can fill our hearts with cherished memories that will bring comfort and warmth long after our loved one is gone.

[**Prompt:** Tell a story about a lasting memory you have with your loved one.]

4.5.2 Discovering Silver Linings and Gratefulness

Tip: *While it may be challenging to see through the veil of illness, there is often a silver lining hidden amidst the difficulties. It could be the way our loved one's strength shines through, the unwavering support from friends and family, or the newfound appreciation for life's simple pleasures.*

In the face of illness, we learn to be grateful for every small victory and to find beauty in the midst of pain. It's about finding solace in the small things – a comforting hug, a genuine smile, or a shared joke. Embracing a mindset of gratitude helps us focus on the positive aspects of our journey and allows us to find moments of joy even in the toughest of times.

[**Prompt:** Share an experience with your loved one that highlights a silver lining or something for which you are grateful.]

4.6. A Lasting Legacy: Lessons Learned and Shared

4.6.1 Valuable Life Lessons Passed Down

Tip: Our loved ones have a way of passing down valuable life lessons that stay with us long after they are gone. Their strength in the face of illness teaches us resilience, their compassion teaches us empathy, and their unwavering love teaches us the power of connection.

By embracing these lessons, we not only honor their memory but also carry their wisdom into our own lives. It's through these teachings that their legacy lives on, shaping our character and guiding us through the challenges we face.

[**Prompt:** Share a valuable life lesson or piece of wisdom that your loved one has passed down to you or others.]

4.6.2 Impact on Family and Community

Tip: The strength displayed by our loved ones during their illness has a profound impact not only on our immediate family but also on our broader community. Their bravery inspires those around them, reminding us of the importance of perseverance and the ability to find light in the darkest of times.

Their legacy lives on through the lives they have touched, spreading strength and resilience like a ripple effect. By sharing their story and the impact they had on those around them, we continue to celebrate their strength and inspire others to face adversity with courage and grace.

[**Prompt:** Share a story that shows our loved one's legacy and impact they had on those around them.]

4.7. Honoring Her Memory: Embracing Grief and Healing

4.7.1 Navigating the Stages of Grief

Grief is a complex and individual journey, and there is no right or wrong way to experience it. When we lose a loved one, it's essential to allow ourselves to feel the full range of emotions that come with grief – from heart-wrenching sadness to anger, confusion, and even moments of peace and acceptance.

Tip: By acknowledging and navigating the stages of grief, we can gradually move through the pain and find healing. It's important to remember that grief is not linear, and it may ebb and flow over time. *Embracing the process and seeking support from loved ones or grief counseling can provide the necessary support to heal and honor our loved one's memory.*

[**Prompt:** Provide some words of comfort and encouragement. Sharing your feelings of grief can be helpful to others who may also be struggling with the same confusing feelings.]

4.7.2 Finding Healing through Support and Remembrance

While grief can feel isolating, it's essential to remember that we are not alone in our journey. Seeking support from friends, family, or support groups can provide immense comfort and understanding during this challenging time. Sharing stories, memories, and emotions with others who have experienced a similar loss can create a sense of community and help us find solace.

Tip: Additionally, finding ways to remember and honor our loved one can be incredibly healing. Creating a memory box, planting a tree in their honor, or participating in activities they loved can be meaningful ways to keep their spirit alive and find comfort as we navigate through our grief.

4.8. Celebrating Life: Continuing the Legacy of Strength and Love

4.8.1 Honoring Her Wishes and Advocating for Awareness

Tip: One way to celebrate the life of our loved one is to honor their wishes and carry forward their passions. If they had a cause they were deeply passionate about, we can become advocates for that cause, raising awareness and contributing to the change they wanted to see in the world.

By channeling our grief into positive action, we can keep their memory alive while making a tangible impact on the issues they cared about. It's a powerful way to honor their legacy and ensure their voice continues to be heard.

[**Prompt:** Identify something that your loved one was passionate about [charity/ advocacy] and make a suggestion to contribute, honor and continue your loved one's legacy.]

4.8.2 Living with Purpose and Carrying Her Spirit Forward

Living with purpose is a powerful way to carry [Name]'s spirit forward. It's about embracing life fully, pursuing our dreams, and finding joy in everyday moments. By living authentically and passionately, we honor my mother's memory and ensure that her spirit continues to light our path.

With her strength as our inspiration, we can face life's challenges head-on and find the courage to choose love, kindness, and compassion in everything we do. It is through our actions and the love we share with others that we keep [Name]'s legacy alive, forever celebrating her strength in the face of illness. In concluding this heartfelt tribute, it is with profound gratitude and love that we honor the memory of my mother. [Name] exemplified strength, grace, and an unwavering spirit that continues to inspire us. As we carry her legacy forward, we find solace in knowing that her love and resilience will forever be etched in our hearts. Though [Name] may no longer be physically present, her light shines brightly, reminding us to celebrate life's precious moments and embrace the strength within ourselves. In loving memory of my mother, may her spirit continue to guide and uplift us all.

5. Eulogy 2 - Honoring the Life of My Father: A Heartfelt Eulogy for a Fighter

5.1 Introduction: Remembering a Remarkable Life

5.1.1 Remembering a Remarkable Life

In this heartfelt eulogy, we gather to honor the life of a remarkable individual, [Name]. I am [Your Name], [Name]'s [Your relationship to the deceased] and I am honored to speak on behalf of the loved ones gathered here today to pay tribute. Through his journey as a fighter, [Name] left an indelible impact on the lives he touched. This eulogy serves as a tribute to his strength, resilience, and unwavering spirit. As we reflect on his early life, triumphs, and challenges, we will uncover the valuable lessons he taught us. We will delve into the profound impact he had on others, the cherished memories we shared, and the bittersweet farewell we bid. Finally, we will explore how we can continue [Name]'s legacy by embracing his courage and perseverance. Let us embark on this heartfelt journey of honoring the life of my father, [Name], a true fighter.

5.1.2 The Loved Ones who Continue His Legacy

Our beloved [Name]'s passing has left a profound void in our lives. In reflecting on his life, it is important to acknowledge those who continue to carry his legacy forward. [Name] is survived by [State and name the close kins e.g. his loving family, including his devoted wife, [Name] and their [number] children [List Names], who were the center of his universe.] [State and name other relatives e.g. He leaves behind a host of cherished relatives, including nieces, nephews, and cousins whom he held dear.] Additionally, he touched the lives of countless friends and acquaintances through his graciousness and unwavering support. His presence will be greatly missed by all who had the privilege of knowing him. Although this loss brings immeasurable grief, we find solace in knowing that [Name] has engendered a lasting impact on those whose lives he gracefully enhanced with love and joy.

5.1.3 An Unforgettable Presence

My father was a force to be reckoned with. From the moment he walked into a room, his presence commanded attention. His booming laugh, his infectious smile, and his unwavering confidence made him someone you couldn't help but notice. [Name] had a way of making everyone feel important, of making everyone feel seen. And now, as we gather here today to honor his life, we remember the remarkable man who touched so many hearts.

5.1.4 The Importance of Honoring His Life

In a world that often moves too fast, where we often forget to pause and reflect on the impact certain individuals have had on us, it is crucial that we take the time to honor my father's life. His was a life well-lived, filled with triumphs and challenges, and it is through remembering and celebrating [Name]'s journey that we find solace and inspiration. It is through sharing our memories and stories that we keep his spirit alive, and ensure that his legacy lives on.

5.2 Early Life and Background: The Making of a Fighter

5.2.1 Childhood Memories and Influences

From a young age, my father displayed an indomitable spirit. Growing up in humble beginnings, he faced numerous obstacles that could have easily deterred him. Yet, it was through these early challenges that he developed the strength and resilience that would become the hallmark of his character. His childhood memories were filled with determination, as he relentlessly pursued his dreams and never allowed setbacks to define him.

5.2.2 Overcoming Adversity: Early Obstacles Faced

Life threw its fair share of curveballs at my father, but he never shied away from a challenge. Whether it was financial difficulties, personal setbacks, or societal expectations, he met each obstacle head-on. [Name] taught us the value of hard work and perseverance, showing us that even when the odds seemed insurmountable, with persistence and a steadfast belief in oneself, anything could be overcome.

5.3 Triumphs and Challenges: A Journey Filled with Resilience

5.3.1 Career Milestones and Achievements

Throughout his life, my father achieved remarkable milestones in his career. From climbing the corporate ladder to starting his own successful business, he was a testament to what could be accomplished through dedication and unwavering determination. He believed that hard work was the key to success and showed us that with passion and a relentless drive, we could achieve greatness.

5.3.2 Battling Health Issues: A Test of Character

In the face of adversity, my father's true character shone through. When he was diagnosed with a serious health condition, he faced it with bravery and an unyielding determination to live life to the fullest. [Name] refused to let illness define him, and instead, used it as an opportunity to appreciate the beauty of each day. His resilience and positive attitude taught us that even in the darkest of times, there is always hope and strength to be found.

5.4. Lessons Learned: My Father's Legacy of Strength and Determination

5.4.1 The Power of Perseverance

Above all, my father's life was a testament to the power of perseverance. He showed us that success is not always about easy wins or smooth journeys. It is about picking ourselves up when life knocks us down, about refusing to give up even when the odds seem insurmountable. [Name]'s unwavering determination serves as a reminder to us all that with grit and resilience, we can overcome any obstacle that comes our way.

5.4.2 Finding Strength in the Face of Adversity

My father's legacy lies not only in his achievements, but also in his ability to find strength and goodness in every situation. He faced adversity with grace and a steadfast belief in the power of positivity. [Name] taught us that even when life throws us curveballs, we have the choice to respond with resilience and unwavering hope. It is this lesson, perhaps above all others, that we carry with us as we say goodbye to a remarkable man who taught us the true meaning of strength and determination.

5.5 Impact on Others: A True Inspiration to All

5.5.1 Touching Lives and Making a Difference

When we think about the impact one person can have on the lives of others, my father's name immediately comes to mind. He was a true inspiration to all who knew him, and even to those who only heard about his story. I have lost count of the number of people who have shared with me how my father's strength and resilience helped them navigate through their own challenges. He showed us that no matter how tough life got, we could always find a way to keep fighting.

5.5.2 An Enduring Influence on Family and Friends

Beyond his impact on the wider community, my father's influence on our family and friends will forever be cherished. He was not only a loving father but also a trusted confidant and a source of unwavering support. His kind heart and infectious laughter brought joy to every gathering, and his wisdom guided us through both good and difficult times. The memories we shared with him will forever remain etched in our hearts.

5.6 Fond Memories: Cherishing the Beautiful Moments Together

5.6.1 Shared Adventures and Heartwarming Stories

Reflecting on the beautiful moments we shared together brings a smile to my face, despite the sorrow in my heart. The adventures we embarked on, the laughter we shared, and the inside jokes only we understood created a bond that can never be broken. From camping trips under the starry sky to impromptu dance parties in the living room, these memories will forever be treasured.

5.6.2 The Unforgettable Bond Between Father and Child

The bond between a father and child is truly unique, and our bond was no exception. My father was not just a parent but also a friend, a mentor, and a role model. He taught me important life lessons, like the value of hard work, determination, and compassion. He was always there to lend an ear and offer advice, even if I didn't always follow it. Our bond lives on in my heart, reminding me of the strength and love I was lucky enough to experience.

5.7 Saying Goodbye: A Farewell to a Beloved Fighter

5.7.1 Celebrating a Life Well-Lived

Today, as we gather to say our final goodbyes to my father, let us not dwell on the sorrow of his absence but instead celebrate the incredible life he lived. [Name] fought battles both big and small, and he did so with unwavering courage and determination. His legacy is not one of defeat but of resilience, reminding us that even in the face of adversity, we can rise above and make a difference.

5.7.2 Honoring His Memory in the Final Goodbye

As we bid farewell to my father, we carry forward the memories, values, and lessons he bestowed upon us. In this final goodbye, let us honor his memory by embracing the strength and perseverance he embodied. Let us find comfort in knowing that his spirit will forever be with us, guiding us through the challenges that life may throw our way.

5.8 Continuing the Legacy: Honoring My Father's Legacy of Courage and Perseverance

5.8.1 Embracing His Values and Life Lessons

To honor my father's legacy, we must carry on the values and life lessons he so passionately believed in. Let us embrace the importance of compassion, empathy, and resilience, and let these qualities shape our interactions with others. By living out these values, we continue his impact on the world and ensure that his memory lives on.

5.8.2 Inspiring Others Through Sharing His Story

One of the most powerful ways to honor my father's legacy is by sharing his story with others. By recounting his battles and triumphs, we inspire those around us to find the strength within themselves to persevere through their own hardships. My father's story serves as a beacon of hope, reminding us all that no matter how daunting the odds may seem, we can overcome them with determination and unwavering belief in ourselves.

As we bring this heartfelt eulogy to a close, we are reminded of the profound impact my father had on our lives. [Name]'s legacy of strength, determination, and resilience will forever guide and inspire us. Though we may feel the pain of his absence, we find solace in knowing that his spirit lives on within each and every one of us. As we continue our own journeys, we will carry his memory in our hearts and honor him by embracing the values he instilled in us. My father, a true fighter, may no longer be with us in physical form, but his presence will forever be felt. We bid our farewell with gratitude, love, and the promise to keep his legacy alive. Rest in peace, dear father.

6. Eulogy 3 - A Eulogy for a Loving Spouse: Honoring the Resilience of My Husband Living with Heart Disease

6.1 Introduction: Remembering a Life Well Lived

6.1.1 Remembering a Life Well Lived

Losing a beloved spouse is an indescribable pain, but it is also an opportunity to reflect on the incredible resilience and strength that they demonstrated throughout their life, particularly when living with heart disease. This eulogy serves as both a tribute to the enduring love shared between us and a testament to the remarkable journey we embarked on together. I am [Your Name], [Name]'s [Your relationship to name] and I am honored to speak on behalf of the loved ones gathered here to pay tribute.

From the moment of diagnosis to the countless challenges we faced, this tribute celebrates the unwavering spirit of my husband and honors his legacy. It is a story of love, loss, and the unbreakable bond that transcends even the most formidable of obstacles.

6.1.2 A Loving Spouse and His Journey with Heart Disease

Losing a loved one is never easy, especially when that person has shown unwavering strength and resilience in the face of adversity. Today, we gather to honor the life of my dear husband, [Name], who lived with unwavering courage, humor, and grace while battling heart disease. His journey serves as an inspiration to us all, reminding us of the power of love, determination, and an indomitable spirit. Let us celebrate the life of a loving spouse who touched our hearts and taught us valuable lessons.

6.1.3 The Loved Ones who Continue [His/Her] Legacy

Our beloved [Name]'s passing has left a profound void in our lives. In reflecting on his life, it is important to acknowledge those who continue to carry his legacy forward. [Name] is survived by [State and name the close kins e.g. his loving family, including his devoted wife, [Name] and their [number] children [List Names], who were the center of his universe.] [State and name other relatives e.g. He leaves behind a host of cherished relatives, including nieces, nephews, and cousins whom he held dear.] Additionally, he touched the lives of countless friends and acquaintances through his graciousness and unwavering support. His presence will be greatly missed by all who had the privilege of knowing him. Although this loss brings immeasurable grief, we find solace in knowing that [Name] has engendered a lasting impact on those whose lives he gracefully enhanced with love and joy.

6.2 The Journey Begins: Discovering the Diagnosis of Heart Disease

It all started with subtle signs that something was amiss. Fatigue, shortness of breath, and occasional chest pain became like uninvited guests in our lives. Concerned, we embarked on a journey to seek medical advice, hoping for reassurance that it was nothing serious. Little did we know that this journey would lead us to the doorstep of heart disease.

The diagnosis came as a shock, shaking the foundation of our lives. Emotions ran high as we grappled with the reality of a chronic condition that would forever change our lives. Fear, sadness, and uncertainty crept into our hearts, but we refused to let them define us. Together, we chose to face this battle head-on, armed with love and a determination to make the most of every precious moment.

6.3 Battling the Unknown: Navigating the Challenges of Living with Heart Disease

Living with heart disease meant navigating uncharted waters, where every step had to be carefully measured and every decision carried weight. Our lives were transformed as we embraced lifestyle adjustments with newfound dedication. Healthy eating became an adventure, exploring new flavors and discovering the joy of nourishing our bodies. Exercise became an essential component of our routine, finding solace in walks hand in hand, cherishing the simple pleasures.

The medication and treatment regimens became an integral part of our lives, a reminder of the battle we faced together. Pills aligned like soldiers on the countertop, each serving as a shield against the relentless progression of the disease. Uncertainty and anxiety lurked in the shadows, but we confronted them with courage, never allowing them to extinguish the flame of hope that burned brightly within us.

6.4 Love in the Midst of Adversity: Witnessing the Resilience of a Loving Spouse

In the midst of adversity, love became our guiding light. My husband's strength and determination shone through every obstacle he faced. [Name] never wavered in his resolve to fight for his health and happiness, inspiring those around him to do the same. His bravery and unwavering spirit were a testament to his character and an inspiration to us all.

As a devoted spouse, I took on the role of providing emotional and moral support. Together, we weathered the storms that heart disease brought upon us. We laughed, we cried, and we held each other tight during moments of vulnerability. Each day was an opportunity to celebrate our love, cherishing the joyous moments and finding solace in the simple pleasures shared.

Today, as we bid farewell to this incredible soul, we remember the love, resilience, and humor that defined his journey. We honor the lessons [Name] taught us - to cherish life's precious moments, to stay strong in the face of adversity, and to love fiercely without hesitation. May his memory forever be a guiding light, reminding us to embrace life with open arms and hearts.

6.5 Unwavering Support: The Role of Caregivers in Managing Heart Disease

Living with heart disease is no easy feat, and the support of a loving caregiver can make all the difference in the world. Caregivers play a crucial role in the journey of someone with heart disease, providing not only physical assistance but also emotional support.

From managing medications and doctor appointments to offering a listening ear during times of frustration and fear, caregivers provide the unwavering support that is essential for managing heart disease. They are there to lend a hand, help with daily tasks, and be a source of strength.

Tip: It's important to remember that caregivers have their own needs too. Balancing personal needs with the needs of their spouse can be challenging at times. It's important for caregivers to take care of themselves, both physically and emotionally, so that they can continue to provide the best care possible.

Seeking support from support groups and resources can be immensely helpful for caregivers. Connecting with others who are going through similar experiences can provide a sense of camaraderie and understanding. Support groups offer a safe space to share struggles, seek advice, and find solace in knowing that you are not alone.

[**Prompt:** Say words of thanks and appreciation to caregivers and support groups that assisted in the care of your loved one.]

6.6 Celebrating Victories: Overcoming Obstacles and Embracing Moments of Joy

Living with heart disease can sometimes feel like an uphill battle, but it's important to celebrate even the smallest victories along the way. Every small win and milestone achieved in the battle against heart disease is worth celebrating.

Whether it's reaching a personal fitness goal, successfully managing medication, or making positive lifestyle changes, these victories deserve recognition. They remind us that progress is possible, even in the face of adversity.

Finding happiness and joy amidst the challenges of heart disease is a true testament to resilience. It's important to seek out moments of joy and hold onto them tightly.

Tip: Whether it's enjoying a favorite hobby, spending quality time with loved ones, or simply relishing in the beauty of everyday life, these moments of happiness can provide a much-needed respite from the difficulties of the disease.

Cherishing shared experiences and triumphs is also an important part of celebrating victories. Taking the time to reflect on the journey together and acknowledging how far you've come can be incredibly empowering and uplifting.

[**Prompt:** Include a story of a time that you and your loved one spent quality time, had moments of happiness or shared cherished experiences together.]

6.7 The Legacy Lives On: Honoring the Memory of a Beloved Husband

When we lose a beloved spouse to heart disease, their impact and influence continue to live on. It's important to remember and honor the legacy they left behind.

Preserving memories and sharing stories help keep the memory of our loved ones alive. Talking about the happy moments, the challenges overcome, and the love shared not only keeps their memory alive but also provides comfort and healing.

Tip: Engaging in activities that keep the memory alive can also be a powerful way to honor a beloved spouse. Whether it's participating in a charity walk in their name, creating a memorial, dedicating a garden, or volunteering for heart health organizations, these actions can serve as a meaningful tribute to their life and the impact they made.

[**Prompt:** Suggest activities that you intend to do to keep alive the memory of your loved one.]

While the pain of loss may never completely dissipate, remembering and honoring our loved ones can bring a sense of peace and connection.

6.8 Inspiring Others: Lessons Learned from a Life of Courage and Determination

A life lived with heart disease is a life filled with courage and determination. Through the challenges faced and the resilience displayed, valuable lessons can be learned by both those living with heart disease and those who love and care for them.

For those living with heart disease, the lessons are clear; resilience, perseverance, and the importance of self-care. They can draw strength from the examples set by their loved ones and find solace in knowing that they too can overcome the obstacles in their path.

Support and understanding for spouses and caregivers are equally important. By sharing their experiences and advocating for heart health, they can inspire others to take action, seek support, and prioritize their own well-being.

The lessons we learn from a life of courage and determination can be powerful motivators for change. By spreading awareness, advocating for heart health, and supporting one another, we can create a community that is resilient and united in the fight against heart disease.

As I bid farewell to my loving spouse, [Name], I am filled with gratitude for the moments we shared and the lessons learned from his courageous battle with heart disease. His resilience, determination, and unwavering love will forever be etched in my heart. May his memory inspire others facing similar challenges to find strength, seek support, and cherish the precious moments of joy amidst adversity. Let us honor [Name]'s legacy by advocating for heart health and supporting those living with this condition. Farewell, my beloved spouse, your spirit will forever guide and inspire me.

Heart Disease FAQ

1. What is heart disease, and what are its risk factors?

Heart disease refers to a range of conditions that can affect your heart's functionality and overall health. There are multiple types, including coronary artery disease, heart failure, and arrhythmias, among others. The leading risk factors for heart disease include high blood pressure, high cholesterol levels, smoking, obesity, diabetes, family history, and a sedentary lifestyle. Understanding these risk factors is essential in preventing heart disease and making informed lifestyle choices.

2. How can I manage heart disease on a daily basis?

Managing heart disease involves various aspects, including medication, lifestyle changes, and regular medical check-ups. Following a heart-healthy diet low in sodium, saturated fats, and cholesterol is vital. Incorporating regular exercise, such as walking or swimming, can significantly improve cardiovascular health. It is also essential to quit smoking and limit alcohol consumption. Additionally, taking prescribed medications as directed by your healthcare professional is crucial in controlling heart disease and its symptoms.

3. Are there any challenges associated with emotional well-being when living with heart disease?

Certainly, living with heart disease can have an impact on your emotional well-being. Feelings of fear, anxiety, stress, and depression are common, as the condition can cause uncertainty about the future. It is important to seek support from family, friends, or professional counselors who can help you manage these emotional challenges. Engaging in stress-reducing activities like meditation or practicing mindfulness can also be beneficial to your overall mental health.

4. How can I prevent heart disease in the first place?

Preventing heart disease is essential, especially for young adults who may not exhibit symptoms but could still be at risk. It starts with incorporating healthy lifestyle choices like maintaining a balanced diet, exercising regularly, limiting alcohol consumption, and avoiding smoking. Additionally, routine check-ups with your primary care physician can aid in identifying potential risk factors or early signs of heart disease. Engaging in these preventive measures can significantly reduce the likelihood of developing heart disease and promote a healthier future.

7. Eulogy 4 - Saying Goodbye to Our Guardian Angel: A Eulogy for a Loved One Fighting Multiple Sclerosis

7.1 Introduction: Remembering a Beloved Guardian Angel

7.1.1 Remembering a Beloved Guardian Angel

In this heartfelt eulogy, we gather to bid farewell to a cherished loved one who fought a courageous battle against Multiple Sclerosis (MS). [Name]'s journey was one of resilience, strength, and unwavering determination. Through [his/her] struggles and triumphs, [he/she] touched the lives of all who knew [him/her], leaving an indelible mark on our hearts.

I am [Your Name], [Name]'s [Your relationship to the deceased] and I am honored to speak on behalf of the loved ones gathered here to pay tribute. As we reflect on [Name]'s life and legacy, we honor [his/her] bravery, celebrate [his/her] impact, and find solace in the memories we shared. Join us as we pay tribute to our guardian angel, who inspired us with [his/her] love, grace, and unwavering spirit in the face of adversity.

7.1.2 Reflecting on His/Her Life and Legacy

In our hearts, we carry the memory of a beloved guardian angel who fought a valiant battle against the merciless foe known as Multiple Sclerosis. As we gather here today, we remember not only the person [he/she] was, but also the legacy [he/she] leaves behind. Through [Name]'s strength and resilience, [he/she] touched the lives of many and inspired us to face our own adversities with unwavering determination.

7.1.3 The Loved Ones who Continue His/Her Legacy

Our beloved [Name]'s passing has left a profound void in our lives. In reflecting on [his/her] life, it is important to acknowledge those who continue to carry [his/her] legacy forward. [Name] is survived by [State and name the close kins e.g. [his/her] loving family, including [his/her] devoted [husband/wife] [Name] and their [Number] children [List Names], who were the center of [his/her] universe.] [State and name other relatives e.g. [He/She] leaves behind a host of cherished relatives, including nieces, nephews, and cousins whom [he/she] held dear.] Additionally, [he/she] touched the lives of countless friends and acquaintances through [his/her] graciousness and unwavering support. [His/Her] presence will be greatly missed by all who had the privilege of knowing [him/her]. Although this loss brings immeasurable grief, we find solace in knowing that [Name] has engendered a lasting impact on those whose lives [he/she] gracefully enhanced with love and joy.

7.2 The Courageous Battle: A Journey with Multiple Sclerosis

Like a formidable opponent, Multiple Sclerosis presented itself in [Name]'s life, bringing with it a myriad of challenges. From the moment of [his/her] diagnosis, [he/she] faced a turbulent journey filled with uncertainty and physical obstacles. Yet, [he/she] refused to let MS define [him/her]. [Name] tackled each day with indomitable spirit, refusing to be defeated by the unpredictable nature of the disease. Through [his/her] journey, [he/she] became warriors, proving that bravery comes not from a lack of fear, but from the strength to face it head-on.

7.3 A Life of Love and Strength: Celebrating His/Her Impact

In the face of adversity, our guardian angel showed us the true power of love and support. [Name] cherished the relationships that surrounded [him/her], finding strength in the embrace of family and friends. Through [his/her] perseverance, [he/she] taught us that even amidst pain and hardship, there is still room for joy. [He/She] found laughter in the smallest moments and the ability to appreciate the beauty that life had to offer. [Name]'s infectious spirit left an indelible mark on those fortunate enough to cross [his/her] path, reminding us all to live each day with a sense of gratitude and purpose.

7.4 The Unwavering Support: Family and Friends by His/Her Side

Throughout this arduous journey, our guardian angel had an army of unwavering support by [his/her] side. The bonds of family grew stronger, [his/her] unity acting as a pillar of strength during the darkest of days. Friendships, too, proved their resilience as they weathered the storm alongside our loved one. And to the caregivers who dedicated themselves to providing care and comfort, their unwavering commitment touched our hearts and eased our burdens. Together, they formed a safety net that ensured our guardian angel never faced this battle alone.

As we say our goodbyes, let us remember the impact our guardian angel had on our lives. While [Name]'s physical presence may be gone, [his/her] spirit of strength, love, and unwavering resilience remains with us forever. We honor [him/her] not with tears of sorrow, but with gratitude for the inspiration [he/she] bestowed upon us. May [his/her] memory continue to guide and uplift us, reminding us that even in the face of life's greatest challenges, we too can find the strength to rise.

7.5 Inspiring Others: Advocacy and Raising Awareness for Multiple Sclerosis

7.5.1 Becoming an Advocate for MS Awareness

Let's face it, our loved one was a warrior during [his/her] battle with Multiple Sclerosis (MS). [Name] faced countless challenges, displaying unwavering strength and courage. Now, it's our turn to carry the torch and become [his/her] voice in advocating for MS awareness.

Becoming an advocate doesn't mean we have to start a revolution or go on a global speaking tour (although, if that's your thing, go for it!). Instead, it's about finding ways to raise awareness within our own communities. Whether it's sharing personal stories, participating in fundraising events, or educating others about the realities of living with MS, every effort counts.

7.5.2 Using His/Her Voice to Educate and Inform

Our loved one's journey with MS has taught us so much about the disease. [Name] became an expert in navigating the complexities of symptoms, treatments, and lifestyle adjustments. Now, it's our responsibility to use [his/her] voice to educate and inform others.

Through [Name]'s experiences, we can share valuable insights with the world. We can raise awareness about the invisible battles that those with MS face every day and dispel misconceptions surrounding the disease. By becoming a source of knowledge and support, we honor [his/her] legacy and ensure that [his/her] voice continues to be heard.

7.5.3 Leaving a Legacy of Advocacy

Our loved one may no longer be physically present, but [Name]'s spirit and determination live on. Leaving a legacy of advocacy means taking [his/her] passion for MS awareness and making it our own. It means continuing the fight, even when it feels overwhelming.

Whether it's starting a support group, organizing fundraising events, or simply sharing information on social media, we can ensure that [Name]'s legacy lives on. And who knows, maybe one day we'll be the guardian angels for others fighting MS, guiding them with the same love and courage that [Name] showed us.

7.6 Cherishing Memories: Shared Moments and Lessons Learned

7.6.1 Precious Memories of Laughter and Joy

Amidst the challenges of MS, [Name] gifted us with countless moments of laughter and joy. Despite the hardships, [he/she] knew how to find the silver linings and turn even the darkest days into ones filled with smiles and laughter.

As we say goodbye, let's cherish these precious memories. Let's hold onto the sound of [his/her] infectious laughter, the warmth of [his/her] smile, and the love that radiated from [his/her] presence. In these memories, [he/she] will forever be with us, bringing light and happiness during the toughest of times.

7.6.2 Learning Life Lessons through His/Her Experience

Living with MS taught [Name] resilience, strength, and the power of embracing each day. Through [his/her] experience, we learned valuable life lessons that will guide us throughout our own journeys.

[**Prompt:** Include a cherished memory of your loved one that shows his/her resilience and strength or has a lasting impact on you.]

[Name]'s unwavering determination to never give up, even in the face of adversity, showed us the true meaning of courage. [His/Her] ability to find joy and gratitude in the smallest of moments taught us the importance of appreciating what we have. And [his/her] love and compassion towards others, despite [his/her] own struggles, reminded us of the power of kindness.

7.6.3 His/Her Impact on Others and the World

[Name]'s impact reaches far beyond our immediate circle. Through [his/her] journey with MS, [he/she] touched the lives of countless others, inspiring them to face their own battles with strength and hope.

As we reflect on [Name]'s life, let's remember the lives [he/she] have touched and the powerful ripple effect of [his/her] actions. [His/Her] legacy lives on in the hearts of everyone [he/she] encountered, reminding us of the profound impact one person can have on the world.

7.7 Saying Goodbye: Honoring His/Her Legacy and Finding Closure

7.7.1 Funeral and Memorial Service: A Celebration of Life

Saying goodbye to our beloved guardian angel is never easy. But as we gather together to honor [Name]'s life, let's not focus on the sadness of [his/her] absence. Instead, let's celebrate the life [he/she] lived and the impact [he/she] had on all of us.

Even though this is a [funeral / memorial service], let's make it a true celebration of [his/her] life. Let's share stories, laughter, and tears as we remember the beautiful soul that graced our lives. And let's find solace in knowing that [his/her] spirit will forever live on in our hearts.

7.7.2 Keeping His/Her Memory Alive through Rituals and Traditions

Although [Name] may be physically gone, we can keep [his/her] memory alive through meaningful rituals and traditions. Whether it's lighting a candle on special occasions, visiting their favorite places, or dedicating a day each year to honor [his/her] life, these acts can provide comfort and solace.

By continuing these rituals, we ensure that our loved one's spirit remains intertwined with our lives. We can create a space where [Name]'s presence is felt, even in [his/her] physical absence, and where [his/her] memory is cherished for generations to come.

7.7.3 Finding Closure and Moving Forward with His/Her Spirit

Finding closure after losing a loved one is a deeply personal journey, and it's different for everyone. It's about allowing ourselves to grieve, to feel the pain of their absence, and to honor the unique bond we shared.

As we navigate this process, let's remember that our loved one's spirit will always be with us. [Name] will continue to guide us, inspire us, and give us the strength to move forward. Though [he/she] may be gone, [his/her] love and presence remain eternal, reminding us that [he/she] will forever be our guardian angel.

7.8 Embracing Life: Carrying On His/Her Strength and Resilience

7.8.1 Living Life to the Fullest in His/Her Honor

In honor of our loved one, let's embrace life with the same passion, strength, and resilience [Name] exhibited. Let's seize every opportunity, chase our dreams, and live life to the fullest.

When we find ourselves facing challenges, let's remember [his/her] unwavering determination and draw strength from [his/her] memory. Let's hold onto [Name]'s spirit as we face our own battles, knowing that [he/she] is by our side, cheering us on every step of the way.

7.8.2 Finding Inspiration in His/Her Courage

Our loved one's battle with MS taught us what true courage looks like. [Name] faced each day with unwavering strength and an indomitable spirit. And now, it's our turn to find inspiration in [his/her] bravery.

When life throws us curveballs, let's remember the battles [he/she] fought and the obstacles [he/she] faced.

As we say our final goodbyes to our beloved guardian angel, we carry [Name]'s spirit within us. [His/Her] fight against Multiple Sclerosis and [his/her] unwavering strength will continue to inspire us in our own battles. We will cherish the memories we shared, the lessons we learned, and the love we experienced. Let us honor [Name]'s legacy by raising awareness for Multiple Sclerosis and advocating for those who continue to fight this relentless disease. Though [he/she] may no longer be with us in person, [his/her] presence will forever remain in our hearts. Rest in peace, dear guardian angel.

Multiple Sclerosis (MS) FAQ

1. What is Multiple Sclerosis (MS)?

Multiple Sclerosis is a chronic autoimmune disease that affects the central nervous system. It disrupts the flow of information within the brain and between the brain and the body, leading to various physical and cognitive symptoms.

2. How does MS impact the lives of those diagnosed?

MS can have a profound impact on the lives of individuals diagnosed with the disease. It can cause symptoms such as fatigue, difficulty walking, numbness or tingling, muscle weakness, problems with coordination and balance, cognitive impairment, and even emotional changes.

3. How can we support someone with MS?

Supporting someone with MS involves being understanding, patient, and empathetic. Providing emotional support, offering assistance with daily tasks when needed, educating ourselves about the disease, and participating in fundraising events or advocacy efforts are meaningful ways to show support.

4. How can we raise awareness for Multiple Sclerosis?

Raising awareness for MS can be done by sharing personal stories, participating in awareness campaigns, organizing fundraising events, and spreading information through social media platforms. It is important to educate others about the challenges faced by individuals with MS and advocate for research and improved accessibility to treatments.

8. Eulogy 5 - A Touching Eulogy for My Beloved Aunt: A Warrior Against Cancer

8.1 Introduction: Remembering the Life and Legacy of My Beloved Aunt

8.1.1 Remembering the Life and Legacy of My Beloved Aunt

In this heartfelt tribute, we gather to remember and honor the life and legacy of my beloved aunt, [Name], a courageous warrior who fought an arduous battle against cancer. I am [Your Name], [Name]'s [Your relationship to the deceased] and I am honored to speak on behalf of the loved ones gathered here to pay tribute.

Aunt [Name]'s story is one of resilience, strength, and unwavering determination, inspiring all who knew her. From her early years, marked by love and cherished memories, to her valiant fight against the formidable adversary of cancer, her journey serves as a beacon of hope and inspiration. Through this eulogy, we pay tribute to her extraordinary spirit, reflect on the impact she made on our lives and the community, and cherish the invaluable life lessons she imparted. Join us as we celebrate the life and legacy of a remarkable individual who exemplified true strength and touched the hearts of all who knew her.

In the realm of extraordinary humans, my beloved aunt stood out like a shining star. Her journey through life was filled with love, laughter, and compassion, but it was also marked by a fierce battle against an insidious enemy: cancer. Today, as we gather here to bid her a heartfelt farewell, let us celebrate the remarkable life she lived and the indelible mark she left on all of us.

8.1.2 The Loved Ones who Continue her Legacy

Our beloved aunt's passing has left a profound void in our lives. In reflecting on her life, it is important to acknowledge those who continue to carry her legacy forward. Our aunt is survived by [state and name her close kins e.g. her loving family, including her devoted husband [Name] and their [Number] children [List Names], who were the center of her universe.] [State and name other relatives e.g. She leaves behind a host of cherished relatives, including nieces, nephews, and cousins whom she held dear.] Additionally, she touched the lives of countless friends and acquaintances through her graciousness and unwavering support. Her presence will be greatly missed by all who had the privilege of knowing her. Although this loss brings immeasurable grief, we find solace in knowing that Aunt [Name] has engendered a lasting impact on those whose lives she gracefully enhanced with love and joy.

8.2 Early Years and the Bond We Shared

8.2.1 A Childhood Filled with Joy and Laughter

As children, my aunt, [Name], and I shared countless moments of joy and laughter. From [include games you played as a child e.g. playing hide-and-seek in the backyard to building epic sandcastles at the beach], our days were filled with boundless energy and endless adventures. It is these cherished memories that will forever bring a smile to my face and remind me of the beautiful soul she was.

8.2.2 Special Moments and Shared Interests

Beyond the carefree days of childhood, my aunt and I developed a bond built on shared interests and genuine passion. We would spend hours immersed in each other's company, [include things you enjoyed together e.g. discussing books, movies, and our mutual love for ice cream. Whether it was exploring new worlds through the pages of a novel or enjoying the simple pleasure of a scoop of chocolate chip cookie dough ice cream], these were the moments that forged an unbreakable connection between us.

8.3 Her Battle Against Cancer: A Warrior's Journey

8.3.1 Diagnosis and Initial Treatment

When cancer cast its dark shadow over her life, my aunt summoned every ounce of strength within her to face the daunting battle ahead. The initial diagnosis was a blow that shook our entire family, but my aunt's unwavering determination to fight back fueled us all with hope. With the support of an incredible medical team, Aunt [Name] embarked on a courageous journey towards recovery.

8.3.2 The Ups and Downs of Chemotherapy

Chemotherapy became a bittersweet companion on this arduous path. Its harsh side effects tested her resolve, but Aunt [Name] soldiered on, refusing to let cancer dictate the terms of her life. Through the ups and downs, she taught us all what it truly means to persevere, finding moments of joy and laughter even in the darkest of times.

8.3.3 Experimental Treatments and Alternative Therapies

Driven by an unwavering spirit, my aunt explored every possible avenue in her quest for survival. From participating in experimental treatments to embracing alternative therapies, she sought out every ray of hope that promised a chance at reclaiming her health. Her bravery in the face of uncertainty was nothing short of awe-inspiring.

8.4 Impact on Family and Community: A Beacon of Inspiration

8.4.1 Support and Encouragement from Loved Ones

Aunt [Name]'s battle with cancer brought our family closer than ever. We rallied around her, providing unwavering support and encouragement in her darkest moments. Whether it was spending hours at her bedside, holding her hand through difficult treatments, or simply making her laugh with silly jokes, we were determined to be a source of strength for her. Aunt [Name] never felt alone in her fight because she had the love and support of her family surrounding her every step of the way.

8.4.2 Her Advocacy for Cancer Awareness and Support Groups

Aunt [Name]'s journey with cancer ignited a passion within her to make a difference in the lives of others facing the same battle. She became a fierce advocate for cancer awareness, tirelessly sharing her story and spreading knowledge about prevention and early detection. She also dedicated herself to supporting various cancer support groups, offering a helping hand and a shoulder to lean on for those who needed it most. Aunt [Name]'s commitment to raising awareness and providing support to others will continue to inspire us long after her passing.

8.5 Cherishing Memories and Life Lessons Learned

8.5.1 Unforgettable Moments We Shared

Our memories with Aunt [Name]'s are filled with laughter, love, and a zest for life even in the face of adversity. From family vacations filled with silly adventures to cozy evenings spent sharing stories over a cup of tea, every moment spent in her presence was treasured. We will forever hold dear the memories of her radiant smile, infectious laughter, and unwavering spirit.

8.5.2 The Wisdom and Guidance She Imparted

Aunt [Name]'s strength and resilience taught us invaluable life lessons that we will carry with us forever. She taught us to face challenges head-on, with grace and determination. She showed us the importance of cherishing every moment and finding joy in the simplest of things. Aunt [Name]'s reminded us to be compassionate, kind, and always willing to lend a helping hand. Her wisdom and guidance will forever shape the way we navigate through life.

8.6 Celebrating Her Spirit and Commitment to Others

8.6.2 Her Philanthropic Efforts and Volunteer Work

Aunt [Name]'s giving nature extended far beyond her fight against cancer. She dedicated herself to numerous philanthropic endeavors, always seeking ways to make a positive impact in the lives of others. Whether it was volunteering at local shelters, organizing fundraisers for charity, or donating her time and resources to those in need, Aunt [Name]'s generosity knew no bounds. Her selflessness is a reminder to us all that we can make a difference, no matter how big or small.

8.6.3 How She Inspired Others to Make a Difference

Aunt [Name]'s unstoppable spirit and unwavering commitment to helping others inspired everyone she encountered. Her determination to create change, even in the face of adversity, inspired those around her to take action and make a difference in their own communities. Aunt [Name]'s legacy lives on through the countless lives she touched, motivating others to follow in her footsteps and leave their own positive mark on the world.

8.7 A - Conclusion: Honoring the Legacy of a True Warrior

As we bid our beloved Aunt [Name] farewell, we celebrate her life and the indelible mark she left on our hearts. Her strength, resilience, and unwavering spirit will forever serve as a beacon of inspiration in our lives. Through her advocacy, philanthropy, and the lasting memories she created, Aunt [Name]'s legacy as a true warrior against cancer will continue to shine brightly.

Though she may no longer be with us in person, her impact on our family, community, and the world will never be forgotten. Rest in peace, dear Aunt [Name], knowing that your light will guide us always.

As we conclude this tribute to my beloved aunt, we are reminded of the profound impact she had on our lives and the lives of those around her. Her unwavering strength, resilience, and commitment to others will forever be etched in our hearts. Though Aunt [Name] may no longer be physically with us, her spirit lives on, inspiring us to face adversity with courage and to cherish every precious moment. Let us carry forward her legacy by embracing the lessons she taught us and continuing her fight against cancer, ensuring that her warrior spirit lives on in our actions. We say goodbye to an extraordinary individual, leaving behind a remarkable legacy that will forever be remembered. Rest in peace, dear aunt, knowing that your love and inspiration will never fade.

8.7 B - Conclusion: The Strength and Resilience that Defined Her

Adversity has a way of revealing one's true character, and in this regard, [Name] was a force to be reckoned with. She faced each setback with unwavering courage and determination, refusing to let cancer define her. Her resilience in the face of unimaginable challenges was a testament to her extraordinary spirit.

Not only did my aunt face the physical challenges brought on by cancer, but she also confronted the emotional turmoil it unleashed. Aunt [Name] taught us that vulnerability is not a weakness but a source of strength. Through her unwavering love and support, she taught us to cherish each precious moment and to find solace in the simple joys of life.

As we bid farewell to my beloved aunt, let us remember Aunt [Name] as a warrior who fought with grace and dignity. She may have lost the battle against cancer, but she leaves behind a legacy of resilience, love, and strength that will forever inspire us. Rest in peace, dear aunt, [Name]. Your spirit lives on in our hearts.

9. Eulogy 6 - In Loving Memory of Our Uncle: Celebrating His Determination in Fighting HIV/AIDS

9.1 Introduction: Remembering Our Uncle's Legacy

9.1.1 Introduction: Remembering Our Uncle's Legacy

As we gather together to commemorate the life of our beloved uncle, we cannot help but reflect on the profound impact he had in the fight against HIV/AIDS. [Name]'s determination, resilience, and unwavering commitment to raising awareness and supporting those affected by the disease serve as an inspiration to us all. In this eulogy, we pay tribute to his memory, celebrating his remarkable journey and the contributions he made to the HIV/AIDS movement. By understanding the disease, recognizing the importance of advocacy, community support, and education, we hope to honor his legacy and continue the fight against HIV/AIDS in his name.

9.1.2 The Loved Ones who Continue the Legacy

Losing a loved one is never easy, but their memory and legacy can live on through the way we choose to remember them. It is essential to honor their life and the impact they had on those around them. [Name] is survived by [State and name the close kins e.g. his loving family, including his devoted spouse [Name] and their [number] children [List Names], who were the center of his universe.] [State and name other relatives e.g. He leaves behind a host of cherished relatives, including nieces, nephews, and cousins whom he held dear.] Additionally, he touched the lives of countless friends and acquaintances through his graciousness and unwavering support. His presence will be greatly missed by all who had the privilege of knowing him. Although this loss brings immeasurable grief, we find solace in knowing that [Name] has engendered a lasting impact on those whose lives he gracefully enhanced with love and joy.

9.1.3 Reflecting on the Impact of HIV/AIDS

HIV/AIDS has touched the lives of countless individuals and families around the world. This devastating disease has shaped communities, challenged healthcare systems, and brought about societal change. It is important to reflect on the impact of HIV/AIDS and acknowledge the ongoing fight against this global health crisis.

9.2 The Impact of HIV/AIDS: Understanding the Disease

9.2.1 A Brief History of HIV/AIDS

HIV/AIDS has been a prominent health issue for several decades. It was first recognized in the early 1980s and quickly became a global concern. The virus, Human Immunodeficiency Virus (HIV), attacks the body's immune system, weakening its ability to fight off infections and diseases. AIDS (Acquired Immunodeficiency Syndrome) is the final stage of HIV infection, characterized by severe immune system damage.

9.2.2 Key Statistics and Facts About HIV/AIDS

Understanding the scale of the HIV/AIDS epidemic is crucial in grasping its significance. According to the World Health Organization (WHO), approximately 38 million people worldwide were living with HIV in 2019. Since the beginning of the epidemic, almost 75 million individuals have been infected, and over 32 million have died from AIDS-related illnesses.

9.2.3 The Global Impact of the Disease

HIV/AIDS has had a profound impact on various aspects of society, including health, economics, and human rights. It has disproportionately affected marginalized communities, with young women and girls, men who have sex with men, and people who inject drugs being particularly vulnerable. Additionally, HIV/AIDS has strained healthcare systems, slowed economic growth, and highlighted the importance of breaking down stigma and discrimination.

9.3 Our Uncle's Journey: A Story of Determination and Resilience

9.3.1 Early Diagnosis and Challenges Faced

When our uncle received his diagnosis, it was undoubtedly a life-altering moment. [Name] faced the initial shock, fear, and uncertainty that come with learning about one's HIV-positive status. Like many others, he encountered challenges such as stigma, discrimination, and lack of access to proper healthcare, which only added to the already difficult journey.

9.3.2 Treatment and Management of HIV/AIDS

Over the years, advancements in medical research have revolutionized the treatment and management of HIV/AIDS. Antiretroviral therapy (ART) has transformed the lives of individuals living with HIV, reducing the virus to undetectable levels and allowing for a near-normal life expectancy. However, the journey to finding the right treatment and managing the virus can still be arduous.

9.3.3 Our Uncle's Personal Struggles and Triumphs

Our uncle's journey with HIV/AIDS was not without its hardships, but he showed immense determination and resilience. [Name] faced adversity with a sense of humor and a zest for life that inspired us all. Through his courage and strength, he demonstrated that a diagnosis does not define a person and that it is possible to live a fulfilling life in the face of a daunting illness.

9.4 Advocacy and Awareness: Our Uncle's Contributions to the HIV/AIDS Movement

9.4.1 The Importance of Advocacy in HIV/AIDS

Advocacy plays a vital role in the fight against HIV/AIDS. It raises awareness, combats stigma and discrimination, and ensures that those living with the virus have access to the necessary resources for treatment and support. [Name] understood the significance of advocacy and devoted himself to making a difference in the lives of others.

9.4.2 Our Uncle's Impact on Raising Awareness

Our uncle's passion for raising awareness about HIV/AIDS was infectious. Through [Name]'s engaging personality and genuine desire to educate, he reached out to schools, community groups, and medical professionals to share his experiences and knowledge. He sparked conversations, challenged misconceptions, and encouraged people to get tested and seek appropriate care.

9.4.3 Collaborations and Partnerships in the Fight Against HIV/AIDS

Our uncle recognized that collaboration is crucial in addressing the complexities of HIV/AIDS. He actively sought partnerships with local organizations, advocacy groups, and healthcare providers. Together, they worked towards common goals, pooling resources and expertise to enhance prevention efforts, improve access to treatment, and support those affected by the disease.

In celebrating o[Name]'s determination in fighting HIV/AIDS, we honor not only his personal journey but also the countless others whose lives have been touched by this relentless disease. By continuing their fight, we strive towards a future where HIV/AIDS is a thing of the past, and every individual affected receives the care, understanding, and support they deserve.

9.5 Community Support: Honoring Our Uncle's Commitment to Helping Others

9.5.1 The Power of Support Networks

When it comes to facing the challenges of HIV/AIDS, having a strong support network can make all the difference. [Name] understood this firsthand and devoted himself to building a community that would support and uplift those affected by the disease. He believed that no one should face HIV/AIDS alone, and he worked tirelessly to connect individuals, families, and organizations to create a network of care and understanding.

9.5.2 Our Uncle's Role in Empowering the HIV/AIDS Community

Our uncle was not only a beacon of hope for those living with HIV/AIDS but also a catalyst for change. [Name] recognized the importance of empowering individuals with knowledge, resources, and tools to overcome the challenges posed by the disease. Through his advocacy work, he encouraged open conversations, promoted empathy, and fought against the discrimination faced by those affected by HIV/AIDS.

9.5.3 Initiatives and Programs Promoting Community Support

To continue his legacy, numerous initiatives and programs have been established to promote community support for those affected by HIV/AIDS. These programs focus on creating safe spaces, providing emotional and practical support, and fostering a sense of belonging and acceptance. From support groups to counseling services, these initiatives aim to alleviate the isolation and stigma often associated with HIV/AIDS, ensuring that no one has to face the journey alone.

9.6 Overcoming Stigma: Breaking Barriers in HIV/AIDS Education

9.6.1 The Role of Stigma in HIV/AIDS

Stigma remains a significant barrier in the fight against HIV/AIDS. Our uncle understood that the prejudice and fear surrounding the disease not only hindered education and awareness but also perpetuated discrimination against those living with HIV/AIDS. [Name] recognized the urgent need to challenge these misconceptions and replace them with empathy, compassion, and understanding.

9.6.2 Our Uncle's Efforts in Combating Stigma

Uncle [Name] was a fierce advocate for eradicating the stigma associated with HIV/AIDS. Through his public speaking engagements, media appearances, and grassroots activism, he worked to educate communities and break down the barriers of fear and ignorance. By sharing his own experiences and dispelling myths, he encouraged people to see beyond the stigma and embrace those affected by the disease with love and support.

9.6.3 Promoting Education and Understanding

Education is a powerful weapon in the fight against HIV/AIDS stigma. In honor of our uncle's dedication, efforts are being made to expand educational programs that provide accurate information about the disease, its transmission, prevention, and treatment. By promoting understanding and empathy, these initiatives aim to create a society that supports and embraces individuals living with HIV/AIDS, free from judgment and discrimination.

9.7 Celebrating Our Uncle's Life: Commemorating His Achievements and Impact

9.7.1 Remembering Our Uncle's Legacy and Contributions

As we celebrate the life of our beloved uncle, it is essential to reflect upon his remarkable legacy and contributions. His unwavering determination and relentless pursuit of justice and equality have left an indelible mark on the HIV/AIDS community. Through his compassion and advocacy, he inspired countless individuals to stand up, speak out, and fight against this devastating disease.

9.7.2 Sharing Stories and Memories

The memories we have of our uncle are cherished treasures that we hold close to our hearts. It is through sharing these stories and memories that we keep his spirit alive. By reminiscing on the moments of joy, strength, and resilience he brought into our lives, we honor his memory and continue to find inspiration in his unwavering dedication.

[**Prompt:** Include a cherished memory of your uncle that has a lasting impact on you.]

9.7.3 Honoring Our Uncle's Impact on the HIV/AIDS Movement

Our uncle's impact on the HIV/AIDS movement cannot be overstated. His tireless efforts to raise awareness, combat stigma, and provide support have saved lives and transformed communities. As we honor [Name]'s memory, let us come together to build upon his foundations, continue his work, and ensure that his legacy shines brightly, guiding us towards a world free from the burden of HIV/AIDS.

In loving memory of our dear uncle, we say goodbye with heavy hearts but also with a renewed sense of purpose. His tireless efforts in fighting HIV/AIDS will forever be etched in our hearts and minds. As we celebrate [Name]'s life and the impact he made, we are reminded that the battle against this disease is far from over. Let us carry forward his determination, passion, and advocacy, continuing to raise awareness, support those affected, and work towards a world free from the grip of HIV/AIDS. Together, we can honor [Name]'s legacy and make a real difference in the lives of countless individuals. Rest in peace, dear uncle, knowing that your fight lives on.

HIV/AIDS FAQ

1. How can we continue to support the fight against HIV/AIDS in honor of our uncle?
There are several ways you can contribute to the ongoing battle against HIV/AIDS. You can participate in fundraising events, volunteer your time with organizations dedicated to HIV/AIDS advocacy and support, or donate to research initiatives aimed at finding a cure. Additionally, spreading awareness, promoting education, and

challenging stigma surrounding the disease can make a significant impact.

2. What are some resources available for those affected by HIV/AIDS?

There are numerous resources available to support individuals affected by HIV/AIDS. Local community organizations, healthcare providers, and government agencies often offer counseling services, support groups, access to medical treatment, and information on prevention and management. Online platforms and helplines also provide valuable resources, including educational materials, emotional support, and guidance on navigating the challenges of living with HIV/AIDS.

3. How can we help reduce the stigma associated with HIV/AIDS?

Reducing stigma surrounding HIV/AIDS starts with education and open conversations. By dispelling myths and misconceptions, promoting empathy and understanding, and sharing personal stories of resilience and strength, we can help break down barriers. Additionally, supporting campaigns and initiatives that challenge stigma, advocating for non-discriminatory policies, and treating individuals living with HIV/AIDS with compassion and respect can contribute to creating a more inclusive and supportive society.

4. How can we raise awareness about HIV/AIDS within our own communities?

Raising awareness about HIV/AIDS within your community can be done through various channels. Organizing informational sessions or awareness events, collaborating with local schools or community centers to include HIV/AIDS education in their curriculum, and utilizing social media platforms to share facts, personal stories, and resources are effective ways to reach a wider audience. Engaging with community leaders, advocating for policies that prioritize HIV/AIDS prevention and support, and supporting local initiatives can also help raise awareness and promote positive change.

10. Eulogy 7 - Honoring the Valiant Efforts of My Brother

10.1 Introduction: A Brief Overview of My Brother's Journey

10.1.1 A Brief Overview of My Brother's Journey

Throughout our lives, we encounter individuals whose relentless dedication and unwavering spirit leave an indelible impact on our hearts and minds. I am [Your Name], and in my life, that person is none other than my brother, [Name]. From the earliest days of our childhood, it was evident that he possessed an extraordinary drive and determination. In this eulogy, we embark on a journey to honor and celebrate the valiant efforts of my brother, exploring the remarkable milestones he achieved, the obstacles he overcame, and the lasting inspiration he has imparted on countless lives. Join me as we delve into the extraordinary story of a true champion.

10.1.2 The Loved Ones who Continue [His/Her] Legacy

Our beloved [Name]'s passing has left a profound void in our lives. In reflecting on his life, it is important to acknowledge those who continue to carry his legacy forward. [Name] is survived by [State and name the close kins e.g. his loving family, including his devoted [spouse] [Name] and their [number] children [List Names], who were the center of his universe.] [State and name other relatives e.g. He leaves behind a host of cherished relatives, including nieces, nephews, and cousins whom he held dear.] Additionally, he touched the lives of countless friends and acquaintances through his graciousness and unwavering support. His presence will be greatly missed by all who had the privilege of knowing him. Although this loss brings immeasurable grief, we find solace in knowing that [Name] has engendered a lasting impact on those whose lives he gracefully enhanced with love and joy.

10.1.3 Growing up with My Brother

Growing up with my brother was like having a human tornado as a sibling. From the moment he could crawl, he was on a mission to explore and conquer everything in his path. Our house was a constant whirlwind of energy, with my brother at the center of it all. His relentless enthusiasm and adventurous spirit set the stage for the valiant efforts he would later exhibit.

10.1.4 Early Signs of His Valiant Efforts

Even as a kid, my brother displayed an uncanny ability to tackle challenges head-on. Whether it was climbing the tallest tree in the neighborhood or fearlessly diving into the deep end of the pool, he never hesitated to push boundaries. It was evident from an early age that [Name] possessed a determination that surpassed the norm. Little did we know then that these were just the first glimpses of the valiant efforts he would undertake in the years to come.

10.2 Early Life and Aspirations: The Foundation of His Valiant Efforts

10.2.1 Childhood Influences and Dreams

As he grew older, my brother's aspirations began to take shape. His heroes were not the typical ones – he didn't idolize sports stars or celebrities. Instead, [Name] admired those who made a difference in the world, the ones who went against the grain and challenged societal norms. Inspired by their stories, he developed a deep desire to leave his own mark on the world, no matter how audacious it seemed.

10.2.2 Educational Pursuits and Ambitions

With a thirst for knowledge and an insatiable curiosity, my brother pursued his education with unwavering determination. [Name] believed that education was the key to unlocking his full potential and making a meaningful impact. From spending countless hours [in the library/online] to pushing the boundaries of his intellectual pursuits, he laid a strong foundation for his valiant efforts by arming himself with knowledge and skills.

10.3 Unwavering Determination: Overcoming Challenges and Adversities

10.3.1 Facing Personal Obstacles Head-On

Life threw its fair share of obstacles in my brother's path, but he never allowed them to deter him. Whether it was a personal setback or a heartbreaking loss, [Name] faced each challenge head-on with unwavering determination. His ability to rise above adversity and find strength in the face of hardship truly exemplified the spirit of valiance.

10.3.2 Triumphs over Professional Challenges

In his professional life, my brother encountered numerous hurdles that would have made others throw in the towel. But not him. He viewed every setback as an opportunity for growth and learning. With his characteristic perseverance, [Name] turned obstacles into stepping stones and transformed challenges into triumphs. His resilience and tenacity were the driving forces behind his valiant efforts in the professional arena.

10.4 Extraordinary Achievements: Recognizing His Remarkable Accomplishments

10.4.1 Recognition and Awards

As my brother's valiant efforts began to bear fruit, the world took notice. [Name] started receiving recognition for his outstanding contributions and achievements. Awards and accolades poured in, not that he ever sought them. These validations served as a testament to his relentless pursuit of excellence and the impact he was making in his chosen field.

10.4.2 Major Milestones and Breakthroughs

Along his journey, my brother reached major milestones and celebrated remarkable breakthroughs. These were the moments when his valiant efforts truly shone. From groundbreaking discoveries to transformative innovations, his ability to push boundaries and challenge the status quo led to extraordinary achievements that left an indelible mark on his field.

In honoring the valiant efforts of my brother, we pay tribute to a person who never settled for mediocrity. Through unwavering determination, [Name] taught us the power of resilience, the importance of chasing our dreams, and the impact we can make when we refuse to be limited by the boundaries society sets.

10.5 Inspiring Others: My Brother's Impact on the Lives of Many

[Name]'s remarkable journey not only touched our family but also inspired countless others. Through his mentoring and empowerment, he made a lasting impact on the lives of many individuals.

10.5.1 Mentoring and Empowering Others

My brother had a unique gift for mentoring and empowering others. [Name] saw the potential in people even when they couldn't see it in themselves. He provided guidance, support, and encouragement to those who needed it most, helping them unlock their hidden talents and achieve their goals. His selflessness and belief in others served as a guiding light for many on their own journeys to success.

10.5.2 Inspirational Stories from Those He Has Helped

The stories of those my brother helped are a testament to his incredible impact. From [Give examples e.g. a struggling artist who found their voice and achieved recognition to a young entrepreneur who turned their passion into a thriving business], the lives he touched are full of inspiring transformations. [Name]'s unwavering belief in their abilities and relentless support propelled them towards greatness, sparking a ripple effect of positivity and achievement.

10.6 Resilience in the Face of Setbacks: Lessons Learned from His Journey

Throughout his journey, my brother encountered setbacks and disappointments. However, he taught us valuable lessons in resilience and the power of a positive mindset.

10.6.1 Overcoming Failures and Disappointments

Failures and disappointments never deterred my brother; instead, they fueled his determination. He showed us that setbacks are inevitable, but how we respond to them determines our success. [Name] embraced failures as opportunities for growth, constantly learning from them and using them as stepping stones to achieve greater things. His unwavering resilience became a source of inspiration for all who knew him.

10.6.2 Adapting to Change and Embracing Growth

Change is a constant in life, and [Name] understood this well. He exemplified the ability to adapt to new circumstances and embrace personal growth. Whether it was learning new skills, exploring different paths, or embracing unfamiliar challenges, he embraced change with open arms. His ability to navigate uncertain waters taught us the importance of flexibility and a willingness to evolve in pursuit of our dreams.

10.7 Honoring His Legacy: Carrying Forward His Valiant Efforts

Though my brother may no longer be with us, his legacy lives on. We honor his memory by continuing the work he started and advocating for the causes he passionately fought for.

10.7.1 Continuing His Work and Advocacy

The best way to pay tribute to my brother is to carry forward his work and advocacy. We strive to uphold the values he held dear and promote the issues that were close to his heart. By continuing [Name]'s efforts, we ensure that his impact is not forgotten and that the positive change he initiated continues to flourish.

10.7.2 Creating Lasting Impact and Legacy Projects

In addition to continuing his ongoing work, we are also dedicated to creating lasting impact and legacy projects that honor his memory. Whether it's establishing scholarships for aspiring individuals in his field or starting initiatives that align with his passions, we aim to leave a lasting imprint that reflects his vibrant spirit and unwavering dedication to making a difference.

10.8 Conclusion: Celebrating the Extraordinary Spirit of My Brother

My brother's valiant efforts and remarkable impact on the lives of others will forever be celebrated. [Name] journey serves as a powerful reminder of the transformative power of mentorship, resilience, and a genuine belief in the potential of others. As we honor his memory, we are inspired to carry his extraordinary spirit forward, making a positive difference in the world, one life at a time.

As we come to the end of this reflective journey, it is with immense pride and gratitude that we celebrate the extraordinary spirit of my brother, [Name]. His unwavering determination, resilience in the face of setbacks, and inspiring impact on others serve as a testament to his character and the indomitable human spirit. Through his valiant efforts, he has not only achieved remarkable accomplishments but also left an enduring legacy for us to carry forward. May his story continue to inspire and remind us of the power we hold within ourselves to overcome any challenge and make a lasting difference in the lives of others. We honor and cherish the footsteps he has left behind, forever grateful for the profound influence [Name] has had on our lives.

11. Eulogy 8 - Farewell to Our Warrior Princess: Reflecting on the Life of a Daughter Who Fought Lymphoma

11.1 Introduction: Remembering a Warrior Princess

11.1.1 Introduction: Remembering a Warrior Princess

Ladies and gentlemen, esteemed family members and friends, it is my solemn duty and privilege today to stand before you as we gather to pay tribute to the life and legacy of our dearly departed. I am [Your Name], [Name]'s [Your relationship to the deceased] and I am honored to speak on behalf of the loved ones gathered here today to pay tribute to our warrior princess who fought Lymphoma. Through this heartfelt eulogy we hope you learn the highs and lows of her diagnosis and treatment, highlighting her unwavering strength, the impact of her courage on loved ones, and the legacy she left behind. Join us as we delve into the inspiring story of a daughter who fought with unyielding determination, leaving an indelible mark on all those who had the privilege of witnessing her courageous fight.

11.1.2 The Loved Ones who Continue [His/Her] Legacy

In a world often consumed by adversity, there are individuals who rise above the challenges and become beacons of strength. One such warrior was our beloved daughter, [Name], whom we lovingly referred to as our Warrior Princess. Though her life was tragically cut short by lymphoma, her journey was a testament to resilience, courage, and unwavering spirit. [Name] is survived by [State and name the close kins e.g. her loving family, including her devoted [spouse] [Name] and their [number] children [List Names], who were the center of her universe.] [State and name other relatives e.g. She leaves behind a host of cherished relatives, including nieces, nephews, and cousins whom she held dear.] Additionally, she touched the lives of countless friends and acquaintances through her graciousness and unwavering support. Her presence will be greatly missed by all who had the privilege of knowing her. Although this loss brings immeasurable grief, we find solace in knowing that [Name] has engendered a lasting impact on those whose lives she gracefully enhanced with love and joy.

11.2 Battling Lymphoma: The Diagnosis and Treatment Journey

The journey of our Warrior Princess began with the unexpected news of a lymphoma diagnosis. Like a bolt of lightning in a clear sky, this revelation shook our world and thrust us into a whirlwind of medical consultations and treatment options. In the early stages, she exhibited signs of fatigue, unexplained weight loss, and persistent night sweats – the telltale signs of something amiss.

After a series of diagnostic tests, the diagnosis was confirmed, and the battle against lymphoma officially commenced. Determined to conquer this formidable foe, our daughter fearlessly explored various treatment options, seeking the best course of action to increase her chances of victory. Every decision was carefully weighed, and every step forward was accompanied by equal parts hope and uncertainty.

Chemotherapy became a recurring chapter in her story, with its own set of challenges. The side effects, the emotional toll, and the physical strain were no match for her indomitable spirit. She faced each session with a mischievous grin and an unwavering determination to come out stronger on the other side. Our Warrior Princess was not one to back down from a fight, even when the odds seemed insurmountable.

11.3 Strength in Adversity: Exploring the Resilience of a Warrior Princess

What set [Name] apart was not just her physical strength but also her remarkable mental and emotional fortitude. In the face of overwhelming challenges, she demonstrated a resilience that left us in awe. It was as if she had tapped into an inner wellspring of strength that allowed her to weather the toughest storms with a smile on her face.

During her battle, she often confided that it was her unwavering determination and positive outlook that kept her going. Even in the darkest moments, she found light. [Name] inspired us all with her ability to find joy in the smallest victories and to never lose sight of hope. Her spirit was infectious, touching the hearts of everyone who crossed her path.

11.4 A Beacon of Hope: The Impact of a Daughter's Courage on Loved Ones

In her battle against lymphoma, our [Name] was not alone. She was surrounded by a circle of unwavering support from family and friends who stood by her side every step of the way. Their love and encouragement were like a lifeline, giving her the strength to persevere in the darkest of times.

But our Warrior Princess's impact extended far beyond her immediate circle. Her unwavering courage and tenacity inspired those who witnessed her battle. Strangers reached out, their own struggles finding solace in her story. She became a beacon of hope to others, showing them that even in the face of adversity, it is possible to fight with unwavering strength and grace.

As we bid farewell to our beloved Warrior Princess, we carry her spirit within us. Her battle may have been cut short, but her legacy lives on in the hearts of those she touched. Through [Name]'s story, we are reminded of the power of resilience, the importance of cherishing every moment, and the indomitable spirit within us all. Here's to our Warrior Princess, may her spirit guide us through the storms that lie ahead.

11.5 Defying the Odds: Celebrating the Triumphs and Milestones

11.5.1 Major Milestones in the Journey

In the battle against lymphoma, every victory is worth celebrating. From completing rounds of chemotherapy to reaching remission, the journey of our warrior princess was filled with major milestones that showcased her strength and resilience. Each step forward was a testament to her unwavering determination and the indomitable spirit that defined her.

11.5.2 Overcoming Setbacks and Celebrating Victories

While the road was undoubtedly challenging, our warrior princess faced setbacks head-on and emerged even stronger. From enduring the side effects of treatment to conquering moments of doubt and fear, she never allowed herself to be defined by her illness. With each setback, [Name] found the inner strength to rise again, reminding us all of the power of perseverance and hope.

11.6 Advocacy and Awareness: Spreading the Legacy of the Warrior Princess

11.6.1 Becoming an Advocate for Lymphoma Research

In [Name]'s honor, we have taken up the mantle of advocacy, continuing the fight she started against lymphoma. By becoming advocates for lymphoma research, we hope to raise awareness about this disease and support organizations working tirelessly to find a cure. Our warrior princess may no longer be with us, but her voice lives on through our determination to make a difference.

11.6.2 Raising Awareness and Funds for the Cause

Through various initiatives and events, we strive to give a voice to those affected by lymphoma and raise awareness about the importance of early detection and treatment. By organizing fundraisers and supporting research efforts, we aim to ensure that others facing this disease have access to the resources and support they need. Together, we can make a significant impact and work towards a future where lymphoma is eradicated.

11.7 Finding Solace: Coping with Grief and Embracing the Memories

11.7.1 Navigating the Grieving Process

Grief is a complicated and personal journey, and each person copes with it in their own way. In the wake of losing our warrior princess, we have found solace in coming together as a community, sharing our stories, and supporting one another. It is through this collective strength that we navigate the grieving process, finding comfort in knowing we are not alone.

11.7.2 Treasuring the Memories of the Warrior Princess

While our warrior princess may have left this world too soon, her memory lives on in our hearts and minds. We cherish the moments we shared, the laughter and the tears, and we hold onto them tightly. Through the memories we carry, she remains a guiding light, reminding us to live each day fully, to love fiercely, and to embrace life's challenges with courage and grace.

11.8 The Legacy Lives On: Honoring the Warrior Princess and Her Legacy

11.8.1 Continuing the Fight against Lymphoma in Her Memory

The legacy of our daughter extends far beyond her time with us. In [Name]'s memory, we vow to continue the fight against lymphoma, supporting those currently battling the disease and working towards a future where no one has to endure its hardships. By fighting for better treatments, increased awareness, and improved support systems, we honor her legacy and ensure that her impact is felt for generations to come.

11.8.2 Keeping Her Spirit Alive through Acts of Kindness and Courage

Acts of kindness and courage were at the very core of our warrior princess's being. To honor [Name], we strive to embody those qualities in our own lives. Whether it's extending a helping hand to someone in need or facing our fears with the same bravery she displayed, we keep her spirit alive by carrying forward the values she held dear. In doing so, we ensure that her impact on the world continues to inspire and uplift those around us.

As we bid farewell to our warrior princess, we carry her spirit of resilience, hope, and advocacy within our hearts. [Name]'s journey serves as a reminder that even in the face of immense challenges, we can find the strength to persevere. May her legacy inspire us to continue the fight against lymphoma, to support those battling the disease, and to cherish the precious moments that life offers. Though she may be physically gone, her impact lives on, forever reminding us of the power of a warrior's spirit.

Lymphoma FAQ

1. What is lymphoma?
Lymphoma is a type of cancer that affects the lymphatic system, which is a part of the body's immune system. It occurs when abnormal lymphocytes (a type of white blood cell) start to grow uncontrollably, forming tumors in the lymph nodes or other lymphatic tissues.

2. How common is lymphoma?
Lymphoma is one of the most common cancers worldwide, with various subtypes. The prevalence of lymphoma can vary depending on the subtype and geographical location. It affects people of all ages, though certain types are more common in specific age groups.

3. What are the treatment options for lymphoma?

The treatment for lymphoma depends on several factors, including the type and stage of the disease. Common treatment options include chemotherapy, radiation therapy, immunotherapy, targeted therapy, and stem cell transplantation. The choice of treatment is personalized based on individual circumstances and may involve a combination of these approaches.

4. How can I support the cause and raise awareness about lymphoma?

There are several ways to support the cause and raise awareness about lymphoma. You can participate in fundraising events organized by lymphoma research organizations, donate to support ongoing research efforts, volunteer your time or expertise to organizations working in the field, and educate others about the signs, symptoms, and treatment options for lymphoma. By spreading awareness, you can contribute to early detection, improved treatments, and support individuals and families affected by lymphoma.

12. Eulogy 9 – Reminiscing About the Beautiful Soul We Lost to Alzheimer's Disease: An Emotional Eulogy

12.1 Introducing the Beautiful Soul: A Life Worth Remembering

12.1.1 Introducing the Beautiful Soul: A Life Worth Remembering

Alzheimer's disease robs us of our loved ones in the cruelest manner, gradually erasing memories, personalities, and the essence of who they once were. In this heartfelt eulogy, we gather to reminisce about a beautiful soul we lost to Alzheimer's disease - a person whose life touched our hearts, whose laughter resonated in our souls, and whose essence will forever be imprinted in our memories. I am [Your Name], [Name]'s [Your relationship to the deceased] and I am honored to speak on behalf of the loved ones gathered here today to pay tribute. Join us as we honor [his/her] life, reflect on the devastating journey [he/she] endured, and find solace and hope in the power of love, resilience, and the beauty of a life well-lived.

12.1.2 A Brief Overview of the Individual's Life

Our story begins with a life that was as vivid and colorful as a painting. This beautiful soul, who graced our lives and hearts, lived a life worth remembering. From humble beginnings to extraordinary adventures, [his/her] journey was a tapestry of experiences that defined the essence of who [he/she] was.

12.1.3 The Loved Ones who Continue [His/Her] Legacy

Our beloved [Name]'s passing has left a profound void in our lives. In reflecting on [his/her] life, it is important to acknowledge those who continue to carry [his/her] legacy forward. [Name] is survived by [State and name the close kins e.g. [his/her] loving family, including [his/her] devoted [husband/wife] [Name] and their [number] children [List Names], who were the center of [his/her] universe.] [State and name other relatives e.g. [He/She] leaves behind a host of cherished relatives, including nieces, nephews, and cousins whom [he/she] held dear.] Additionally, [he/she] touched the lives of countless friends and acquaintances through [his/her] graciousness and unwavering support. [His/Her] presence will be greatly missed by all who had the privilege of knowing [him/her]. Although this loss brings immeasurable grief, we find solace in knowing that [Name] has engendered a lasting impact on those whose lives [he/she] gracefully enhanced with love and joy.

12.1.4 Personal Qualities and Accomplishments

This extraordinary individual possessed an infectious zest for life. [Name]'s laughter could light up a room, and [his/her] kindness knew no bounds. [He/She] was the epitome of resilience and determination, conquering obstacles with grace and strength. [Name]'s accomplishments, both big and small, added color to the canvas of [his/her] life and left an indelible mark on those fortunate enough to cross [his/her] path.

12.2 The Devastating Journey with Alzheimer's Disease

12.2.1 Diagnosis and Early Symptoms

Life had a cruel twist in store for our beloved one as [he/she] was diagnosed with Alzheimer's disease. It started with subtle signs, moments of forgetfulness that we all brushed off as a normal part of aging. Little did we know that these innocent lapses were harbingers of the devastation that awaited us.

12.2.2 Progression of the Disease

Like an unrelenting storm, Alzheimer's took its toll on our loved one. Memories, once crystal clear, became fragments lost in a foggy abyss. Simple tasks that were once second nature became insurmountable challenges. We watched helplessly as the disease stripped away layers of [Name]'s identity, leaving us longing for the person [he/she] once was.

12.2.3 Emotional and Physical Toll on the Individual

Alzheimer's snatched away not only memories but also the vibrant spirit that once defined our beloved. It was heartbreaking to witness [Name]'s confusion and frustration as [he/she] struggled to grasp reality. [His/Her] physical decline mirrored the emotional toll the disease took, leaving our hearts heavy with sorrow.

12.3 Cherished Memories: A Testament to a Life Well-Lived

12.3.1 Recounting Happy Moments and Milestones

Amidst the devastating cloud of Alzheimer's, we choose to remember the beautiful moments that defined our loved one's life. From joyous celebrations to quiet moments of togetherness, we hold onto these cherished memories tight. The milestones [Name] achieved, the laughter [he/she] shared, and the love [he/she] imparted will forever serve as a testament to a life well-lived.

12.3.2 Impact on Family and Friends

[Name]'s battle with Alzheimer's not only affected [him/her] but also the web of connections [he/she] had nurtured throughout [his/her] life. Family and friends rallied together, providing support, love, and understanding. Together, we formed a shield of strength, guarding against the disease's relentless assault. Our unity was a testament to the profound impact this beautiful soul had on each of us.

12.4 Reflecting on the Impact of Alzheimer's on Loved Ones

12.4.1 Emotional Struggles and Coping Mechanisms

Alzheimer's left an indelible mark on all those close to our beloved. The emotional struggles were profound, ranging from sadness and grief to frustration and helplessness. Amidst the storm, we found solace in small moments of connection and sought comfort in the support of one another. Laughter became an essential armor, helping us navigate the challenging road ahead.

12.4.2 Shifts in Family Dynamics and Relationships

Alzheimer's taught us the importance of adaptability and resilience within our family dynamics. Roles shifted, and new bonds formed as we adjusted to the evolving needs of our loved one. We learned to celebrate even the smallest victories and cherish the moments of clarity that Alzheimer's couldn't steal. Our relationships grew stronger through the shared burden and the unwavering love that united us.

In reminiscing about the beautiful soul we lost to Alzheimer's disease, we honor [Name]'s memory by carrying forward the love, strength, and resilience [he/she] embodied. Though Alzheimer's may have stolen precious memories, it could never extinguish the light of [his/her] spirit, which continues to shine brightly within us all.

12.5 A Heartfelt Eulogy: Honoring the Strength and Resilience

12.5.1 Expressing Love, Gratitude, and Farewell

Saying goodbye is never easy, especially when we are bidding farewell to someone who has touched our lives so profoundly. In this heartfelt eulogy, we gather to honor the strength and resilience of the beautiful soul we lost to Alzheimer's disease. We express our love, gratitude, and bid our final farewell to a person who, despite their memory fading, left an indelible mark on our hearts.

12.5.2 Sharing Inspiring Stories and Lessons Learned

As we gather here today, reminiscing about the life of our dearly departed, we are reminded of the inspiring stories and valuable lessons [Name] taught us. Even in the midst of a challenging battle with Alzheimer's, [Name] showed us that strength can be found in the smallest of victories and joy can be embraced in the simplest of moments. [His/Her] journey has taught us the importance of cherishing every memory and living life to the fullest.

[**Prompt:** Include a cherished memory of your loved one that has a lasting impact on you.]

12.6 Finding Solace in the Beauty of a Life Remembered

12.6.1 Embracing Grief and Finding Comfort

In the face of loss, grief consumes us, but in this moment, let us find solace in the beauty of a life well-lived. Though Alzheimer's may have stolen some of [Name]'s memories, it cannot take away the essence of who [he/she] was and the impact [he/she] had on our lives. Let us embrace our grief, and find comfort in the knowledge that [Name]'s spirit lives on in our hearts and in the memories we hold dear.

12.6.2 Preserving and Passing on the Legacy

As we gather to honor our loved one's memory, let us remember that a legacy is not just about the individual, but about the lives they touched. It is our responsibility to preserve and pass on the lessons and values they imparted to us. By sharing their story and the impact they had on our lives, we keep their spirit alive and ensure that their legacy lives on through us.

12.7 Spreading Awareness: The Fight Against Alzheimer's Disease

12.7.1 Advocacy and Support Initiatives

While we may be gathered here today mourning the loss of our loved one, let us also take a moment to turn our grief into action. Alzheimer's disease is a relentless foe, affecting millions of lives worldwide. By advocating for increased funding and support, we can contribute to the ongoing fight against this devastating disease. Together, let us become voices of change and work towards a future where Alzheimer's is a thing of the past.

12.7.2 Resources for Alzheimer's Education and Research

Knowledge is power, and in the fight against Alzheimer's, education and research are crucial. There are numerous organizations, such as [Name Alzheimer's Association], that provide valuable resources for families affected by this disease. Whether it is information about caregiving, support groups, or advancements in research, these resources can help us navigate the challenges posed by Alzheimer's and provide a glimmer of hope for a brighter future.

12.8 Embracing Love and Loss: Moving Forward with Hope and Compassion

12.8.1 Celebrating Life and Healing Together

Though the pain of loss may remain, let us remember that love is a balm that heals. As we navigate the path forward, let us celebrate the life we were fortunate to witness and the love we shared with our departed loved one. Together, we can find solace in each other's presence, embracing the love that binds us and finding strength in unity.

12.8.2 Encouraging Others to Share their Stories and Seek Support

In sharing our own stories of loss and the impact of Alzheimer's disease, we create a space where others can find solace and support. Let us encourage those who may be walking a similar path to seek out the comfort of community, knowing that they are not alone in their grief. By sharing, listening, and offering compassion, we can help lighten the burden and bring a glimmer of hope to those in need.

12.8.3 Embracing Love and Loss: Moving Forward with Hope and Compassion

As we conclude, we are reminded that while Alzheimer's disease may have taken away our loved one, it cannot erase the love and impact [Name] had on our lives. We must continue to spread awareness, support research efforts, and offer compassion to those affected by this devastating disease. May we find solace in the cherished memories, the lessons learned, and the strength that our loved one exemplified throughout [his/her] journey. Let us move forward with hope, celebrating [his/her] life, and carrying [his/her] legacy of love and resilience in our hearts.

Alzheimer's FAQ

1. Can Alzheimer's disease be prevented or cured?

Currently, there is no known cure for Alzheimer's disease. However, leading a healthy lifestyle, engaging in mentally stimulating activities, and maintaining social connections may help reduce the risk or delay the onset of the disease. Ongoing research is focused on finding effective prevention and treatment strategies.

2. How can I support a loved one with Alzheimer's?

Caring for someone with Alzheimer's disease can be challenging, but there are several ways to provide support. Educate yourself about the disease, join support groups, and seek guidance from healthcare professionals. Show patience, empathy, and understanding, and create a safe and supportive environment. Offering emotional support and engaging in activities that promote cognitive stimulation can also be beneficial for your loved one.

3. Are there resources available for Alzheimer's patients and their families?

Yes, there are numerous resources available for Alzheimer's patients and their families. Organizations such as the Alzheimer's Association offer information, support groups, and helplines to provide assistance and guidance. Additionally, there are online communities, caregiver support programs, and respite care services that offer relief and support for families caring for individuals with Alzheimer's.

4. How can I get involved in the fight against Alzheimer's disease?

There are various ways to get involved in the fight against Alzheimer's disease. You can participate in fundraising events, volunteer for clinical trials or research studies, or donate to organizations dedicated to Alzheimer's research and support.

Additionally, spreading awareness about the disease, advocating for policy changes, and supporting caregivers and individuals affected by Alzheimer's are vital ways to make a difference.

13. Eulogy 10 - Paying Tribute to My Grandfather: An Inspirational Eulogy for a Man Who Battled Stroke

13.1 Introduction: Remembering a Remarkable Life

13.1.1 Remembering a Remarkable Life

The passing of a loved one is an opportunity to reflect on the impact they had on our lives. I am [Your Name], [Name]'s [Your relationship to the deceased] and I am honored to speak on behalf of the loved ones gathered here today to pay our respects. In this heartfelt eulogy, we pay tribute to my grandfather, a man who battled stroke with unwavering courage and resilience. Through his remarkable journey, he not only overcame adversity but also left an indelible mark on our family, friends, and community. This eulogy serves as a tribute to his inspiring life, recounting his early accomplishments, his battle with stroke, the lessons he taught us, and the lasting legacy he leaves behind. Join us as we remember and celebrate the life of a truly extraordinary man.

In this eulogy, we gather today to pay tribute to a truly remarkable man, my grandfather, [Name]. He was not just a grandfather, but a source of inspiration and strength for our entire family. Though his battle with stroke was long and challenging, it is important for us to remember the incredible life he lived and the impact he had on all those fortunate enough to know him. Today, we celebrate his resilience, his achievements, and the lasting lessons he leaves behind.

13.1.2 The Loved Ones who Continue [His/Her] Legacy

Our beloved [Name]'s passing has left a profound void in our lives. In reflecting on his life, it is important to acknowledge those who continue to carry his legacy forward. [Name] is survived by [State and name the close kins e.g. his loving family, including his devoted spouse, [Name] and their [number] children [List Names], who were the center of his universe.] [State and name other relatives e.g. He leaves behind a host of cherished relatives, including nieces, nephews, and cousins whom he held dear.] Additionally, he touched the lives of countless friends and acquaintances through his graciousness and unwavering support.

His presence will be greatly missed by all who had the privilege of knowing him. Although this loss brings immeasurable grief, we find solace in knowing that [Name] has engendered a lasting impact on those whose lives he gracefully enhanced with love and joy.

13.2 Early Life and Achievements: A Glimpse into Grandfather's Journey

13.2.1 Childhood Influences: Shaping Values and Ambitions

As a child, my grandfather experienced various influences that shaped his values and ambitions. Growing up in a humble household, he learned the importance of hard work, compassion, and determination. These principles would guide him throughout his life, propelling him towards greatness.

13.2.2 Educational Pursuits: Grandfather's Academic Success

Education was always a priority for my grandfather. He dedicated himself to his studies, excelling academically and earning numerous accolades along the way. His thirst for knowledge was insatiable, and he never stopped learning and seeking new opportunities to expand his horizons.

13.2.3 Professional Milestones: Grandfather's Career Accomplishments

In his professional life, my grandfather achieved remarkable success. Through his unwavering commitment and unparalleled work ethic, he climbed the ladder of success, reaching unprecedented heights in his career. His determination and passion were truly inspiring, leaving a lasting legacy in his field.

13.3 The Battle with Stroke: Overcoming Adversity and Finding Strength

13.3.1 The Onset of the Stroke: A Life-Altering Moment

The onset of my grandfather's stroke was a life-altering moment for our entire family. Overnight, everything changed. But true to his nature, he faced this immense adversity head-on, refusing to let it define him. Instead, he showed us the true strength of the human spirit.

13.3.2 Medical Challenges: Navigating Treatment and Rehabilitation

Throughout his battle with stroke, my grandfather faced countless medical challenges. From grueling treatments to demanding rehabilitation, he courageously persevered, never letting despair consume him. His determination to regain his health and independence was awe-inspiring to witness.

13.3.3 Family Support and Unwavering Determination

During this difficult time, our family rallied together to support my grandfather every step of the way. We became a united front, offering love, encouragement, and unwavering determination. Together, we fought alongside him, reminding him that he was never alone in his battle.

13.4 Lessons Learned: Grandfather's Impact on Family, Friends, and Community

13.4.1 Resilience in the Face of Adversity: Grandfather's Inspirational Attitude

Throughout his life, my grandfather exemplified resilience in the face of adversity. His unwavering positive attitude and determination to overcome any obstacle were truly inspiring. [Name] taught us that setbacks are not the end, but rather opportunities for growth and personal transformation.

13.4.2 Empowering Others: Grandfather's Mentoring and Guidance

[Name]'s impact extended far beyond our immediate family. He touched the lives of many through his mentorship and guidance. Always ready to offer words of wisdom and support, he empowered others to believe in themselves and reach for their dreams. His legacy of uplifting others will forever remain in the hearts of those he inspired.

13.5 A Life of Resilience and Perseverance: Inspiring Others to Never Give Up

[Name]'s life was a testament to resilience and perseverance, showing us that no matter the challenges we face, we must never give up. Despite battling stroke, he remained determined to live life to the fullest and inspire those around him.

13.5.1 Overcoming Obstacles: Grandfather's Willpower and Fortitude

In the face of adversity, Grandfather exhibited an unwavering willpower and immense fortitude. [Name] refused to let his stroke define him or limit his capabilities. Instead, he tackled each obstacle with determination and proved that our limitations are only as strong as we allow them to be.

13.5.2 Spreading Hope and Encouragement: Grandfather's Advocacy Work

[Name]'s journey inspired him to become an advocate for stroke survivors, spreading hope and encouragement to others facing similar challenges. Through his advocacy work, he provided a voice for those struggling with stroke recovery, empowering them to persevere and find strength in their own stories.

13.6 Fond Memories and Heartwarming Stories: Celebrating Grandfather's Legacy

As we pay tribute to Grandfather, we reminisce about the fond memories and heartwarming stories that define his remarkable legacy. These cherished moments remind us of the impact he had on our lives.

[**Prompt:** Include a cherished memory of your grandfather that has a lasting impact on you.]

13.6.1 Family Bonding and Traditions: Treasured Moments with Grandfather

Grandfather cherished family above all else, and his love brought us together in countless special moments. From holiday gatherings to summer vacations, we shared laughter, love, and created timeless memories that will forever warm our hearts.

13.6.2 Laughter and Joy: Grandfather's Sense of Humor and Playfulness

One of the most endearing qualities Grandfather possessed was his incredible sense of humor and playfulness. No family gathering was complete without his infectious laughter and witty remarks. He had a remarkable ability to find joy in the simplest of moments and taught us all the importance of laughter and levity.

[**Prompt:** Include a cherished memory of your grandfather that shows his humor and playfulness.]

13.7 Honoring the Legacy: Carrying Forward Grandfather's Values and Ideals

To truly honor Grandfather's memory, we must strive to carry forward his values and ideals. By embodying the principles he held dear, we can ensure that his legacy lives on.

13.7.1 Embracing Grandfather's Legacy: Upholding his Principles

Grandfather lived a life guided by strong principles such as integrity, kindness, and compassion. It is now our responsibility to embrace and uphold these values in our own lives. By doing so, we keep his spirit alive and continue the legacy he worked so hard to build.

13.7.2 Paying it Forward: Continuing Grandfather's Philanthropic Endeavors

Grandfather had a deep sense of philanthropy and believed in the power of giving back to his community. We can honor his memory by continuing his philanthropic endeavors, supporting causes that were close to his heart. By making a positive impact on the lives of others, we carry on his selfless nature and the love he had for those in need.

13.8 A – Conclusion: A Lasting Tribute to an Extraordinary Man

As we say our farewells, let us remember Grandfather not for the challenges he faced, but for the extraordinary man he was. Through his resilience, advocacy, and unwavering love for his family, he leaves a lasting legacy that will forever inspire us. May his life remind us to never give up, cherish the moments that bring us joy, uphold our values, and make a positive impact on the world. Farewell, dear Grandfather, your spirit will forever be with us.

13.8 B - Conclusion: A Lasting Tribute to an Extraordinary Man

As we bid farewell to my beloved grandfather, we carry with us the invaluable lessons he taught us through his resilience and perseverance. His life serves as a guiding light, reminding us to never give up in the face of adversity and to always embrace the power of hope and determination. We will honor his legacy by embodying his values and ideals, and by sharing his story of strength and inspiration with others. Though he may no longer be with us, his spirit will forever live on in our hearts. Rest in peace, dear grandfather, knowing that your impact on our lives will never be forgotten.

13.8 C - Conclusion: A Lasting Tribute to an Extraordinary Man

My grandfather's battle with stroke was undoubtedly a challenging journey. However, his life was so much more than the obstacles he faced. Today, as we bid him farewell, let us remember the remarkable man he was, the achievements he accomplished, and the valuable lessons he taught us. May his spirit of resilience and determination continue to guide us as we navigate life's challenges. Farewell, dear grandfather. Your legacy lives on in our hearts.

Stroke FAQ

1. What is a stroke and what are its long-term impacts?
A stroke occurs when blood flow to the brain is disrupted, leading to damage in the affected area. This can result in various physical, cognitive, and emotional changes for the individual. Common challenges faced after a stroke include weakness or paralysis on one side of the body, difficulty with speech or swallowing, memory problems, and emotional changes such as depression or anxiety.

2. Is there anything that can help survivors of stroke? Rehabilitation plays a vital role in helping stroke survivors regain as much independence as possible. Depending on their specific needs, rehabilitation may include physical therapy, occupational therapy, speech therapy, and psychological support. These interventions are designed to improve mobility, restore speech and language skills, address cognitive limitations, and promote emotional well-being.

3. Can stroke survivors return to their previous lifestyle after experiencing a stroke?

The answer is both yes and no. While it may not be possible to revert entirely to life before the stroke, many stroke survivors can lead fulfilling lives with appropriate modifications. Adjustments may be necessary, such as making the home more accessible, using mobility aids, or utilizing assistive technologies. It is crucial to recognize that recovery is a journey, and progress may take time.

4. How to provide support to a loved one who has had a stroke?

Providing care to a stroke survivor requires both physical and emotional support. Offering assistance with daily activities such as bathing, dressing, or meal preparation is vital. Additionally, being a compassionate listener and providing emotional support during challenging moments can significantly impact their emotional well-being. It is important to remember that caregiving can be demanding, and seeking support for oneself is equally essential to avoid burnout.

5. Can stroke survivors prevent another stroke from occurring?

While the risk of recurrence is a concern, there are several steps that can be taken to reduce the likelihood. Lifestyle modifications, such as adopting a healthy diet, engaging in regular physical activity, managing stress levels, and quitting smoking, can significantly decrease the risk of further strokes. Additionally, following prescribed medication regimens and attending regular check-ups with healthcare professionals are crucial in optimizing their health and managing any underlying medical conditions.

14. Eulogy 11 - Commemorating the Resilience and Bravery of our Cousin, Lost to Muscular Dystrophy

14.1 Introduction: Remembering the Life and Journey of our Cousin

14.1.1 Remembering the Life and Journey of our Cousin

Losing a loved one to a debilitating illness is a heartbreaking experience that no family wishes to endure. I am [Your Name], [Name]'s [Your relationship to the deceased] and I am honored to speak on behalf of the loved ones gathered here today to pay tribute. In the case of our cousin, who bravely battled muscular dystrophy, [his/her] journey serves as a testament to resilience and bravery. This eulogy aims to commemorate [his/her] life, shedding light on the impact of muscular dystrophy and the challenges faced by those affected. Through understanding the disease, sharing personal stories, and exploring avenues of support and advocacy, we honor [his/her] memory while spreading awareness about muscular dystrophy and the ongoing efforts to find a cure. Join us as we pay tribute to the indomitable spirit of our cousin.

14.1.2 Early Life and Diagnosis

Our cousin's journey began like any other child's - full of laughter, mischief, and dreams of conquering the world. However, at the age of [Number], [his/her] life took an unexpected turn when [he/she] was diagnosed with Muscular Dystrophy. This rare and debilitating genetic disorder would shape [his/her] life in ways we could never have imagined.

14.1.3 Family Support and Love

Throughout [his/her] battle with Muscular Dystrophy, our [Name] never walked alone. Our family rallied around [him/her], providing unwavering support, endless love, and heaps of laughter. From helping him with everyday tasks to being [his/her] cheerleaders during medical appointments, we stood united, determined to make each day as joyful as possible.

The passing of our dear [Name] has left a huge void in our lives. As we reflect on [his/her] life, it's important to recognize the people who are continuing [his/her] legacy. [Name] is survived by [his/her] loving family, including [his/her] devoted spouse [Name] and their [number] children [List Names], who meant the world to them. [Name] also leaves behind a cherished group of relatives, like nieces, nephews, and cousins, who held a special place in [his/her] heart. Moreover, [he/she] touched the lives of countless friends and acquaintances through [his/her] kindness and unwavering support. Everyone who had the privilege of knowing [Name] will deeply miss [his/her] presence. While this loss brings immense grief, we find comfort in knowing that [Name] has left a lasting impact on those whose lives [he/she] filled with love and joy.

14.2 Battling Muscular Dystrophy: Our Cousin's Strength and Courage

14.2.1 Treatment and Management Strategies

[Name]'s journey through Muscular Dystrophy was filled with medical appointments, therapy sessions, and a myriad of treatments aimed at managing symptoms and slowing the progression of the disease. From physical therapy to specialized medications, [he/she] faced each challenge head-on with strength and determination.

14.2.2 Physical and Emotional Challenges

Battling Muscular Dystrophy means grappling not only with physical limitations but also with emotional hurdles. [Name] faced countless frustrations, moments of despair, and the constant adjustment to a changing body. Yet, [he/she] never let Muscular Dystrophy define [him/her], choosing instead to celebrate each small victory and find joy in life's simple pleasures.

14.2.3 Adaptive Equipment and Assistive Technologies

As the disease progressed, our cousin relied on adaptive equipment and assistive technologies to maintain [his/her] independence and quality of life. From powered wheelchairs to speech-assistance devices, these tools became [his/her] allies in navigating a world that often overlooked the needs of those with disabilities.

14.3 The Impact on Family and Loved Ones: Coping with Loss and Grief

14.3.1 Emotional Roller Coaster of the Disease

Muscular Dystrophy took its toll not only on our cousin but also on our family. It was an emotional roller coaster, with moments of hope, resilience, and laughter blending with times of sadness, frustration, and grief. Each step of the journey was a reminder of the preciousness of life and the strength of our bonds.

14.3.2 Caregiving and Support Networks

Throughout the years, our family became a tight-knit caregiving unit, providing the support our cousin needed while also relying on the love and understanding of friends and support networks. We learned that asking for help is not a sign of weakness but a testament to the strength of our love for our cousin.

14.3.3 Bereavement and Healing

[Name]'s battle with Muscular Dystrophy came to an end, leaving our hearts forever changed. The grieving process has been a mix of tears and cherished memories, but we find solace in knowing that [his/her] spirit lives on in the lessons [he/she] taught us about resilience, bravery, and the importance of cherishing every moment we have together.

14.4 Raising Awareness: Advocacy and Support for Muscular Dystrophy

14.4.1 Educating the Community

When it comes to rare diseases like Muscular Dystrophy, knowledge is power. By educating our community about this condition, we can break down misconceptions and promote understanding. From organizing informative talks and workshops to sharing accurate information on social media, we can help create a more inclusive environment for individuals living with Muscular Dystrophy.

14.4.2 Fundraising and Donations

Raising funds is not just about showing off our impressive bake sale skills (although that's always a plus). By organizing fundraisers and seeking donations, we can support research initiatives, provide financial assistance to families affected by Muscular Dystrophy, and contribute to improving accessibility. So, let's put on our creative hats and find fun and engaging ways to gather support!

14.4.3 Partnering with Muscular Dystrophy Organizations

Sometimes, the best way to make a bigger impact is by joining forces. By seeking partnerships with established Muscular Dystrophy organizations, we can leverage their knowledge, resources, and networks to amplify our efforts. Together, we can advocate for policy changes, organize awareness campaigns, and provide a stronger support system for those living with Muscular Dystrophy.

14.5 Inspiring Stories: Sharing the Triumphs and Triumphs of Muscular Dystrophy Warriors

14.5.1 Overcoming Challenges and Achievements

Muscular Dystrophy may present numerous challenges, but it also breeds incredible strength and resilience. By sharing stories of individuals who have triumphed over adversity, we can inspire hope and foster a sense of community. These stories serve as a reminder that Muscular Dystrophy does not define one's worth or potential.

14.5.2 Advocacy and Activism

From pushing for better healthcare facilities to fighting for inclusive policies, individuals affected by Muscular Dystrophy have been at the forefront of advocacy and activism. By shining a spotlight on their achievements, we not only celebrate their remarkable efforts but also encourage others to join the cause and make a difference.

14.5.3 Support Networks and Community

Building a supportive community is instrumental in navigating the challenges of Muscular Dystrophy. Sharing stories of support networks and highlighting resources available for individuals and families affected by the condition can help connect people, provide comfort, and offer a sense of belonging. Together, we can create a strong and caring network that uplifts everyone.

14.6 Spreading Hope and Encouragement: Resources for Individuals and Families Affected by Muscular Dystrophy

14.6.1 Support Groups and Counseling Services

Living with Muscular Dystrophy can be overwhelming at times, which is why support groups and counseling services are essential. These resources provide a space for individuals and families to share their experiences, seek guidance, and find solace in the company of others who understand their journey.

14.6.2 Accessible Activities and Adaptive Equipment

Living with a condition like Muscular Dystrophy doesn't mean missing out on fun and fulfilling experiences. By promoting accessible activities and highlighting adaptive equipment, we can empower individuals with Muscular Dystrophy to explore their passions and live life to the fullest.

14.6.3 Coping Strategies and Self-Care Tips

Taking care of oneself is crucial for individuals and families affected by Muscular Dystrophy. Sharing coping strategies, self-care tips, and resources for managing physical and emotional well-being can provide much-needed support and empower individuals to prioritize their health and happiness.

Remember, even the smallest acts of support can make a significant impact. Let's come together, celebrate our cousin's resilience, and continue to shine a light on Muscular Dystrophy, spreading awareness, hope, and encouragement to all.

As we come to the end of this eulogy, we are reminded of the enduring strength and bravery exhibited by our [Name] throughout his battle with muscular dystrophy. [His/Her] legacy lives on through the memories we hold dear and the inspiration [he/she] continues to provide. Let us vow to raise awareness, support research, and advocate for those affected by this relentless disease. Together, we can commemorate the resilience of [Name] and work towards a future where muscular dystrophy is no longer a threat. May [his/her] courage and determination serve as a guiding light for others facing similar challenges. We will carry [his/her] spirit with us always.

Muscular Dystrophy FAQ

1. What is muscular dystrophy?
Muscular dystrophy is a group of genetic disorders characterized by progressive muscle weakness and degeneration. It is caused by mutations in genes that are responsible for producing proteins essential for healthy muscle function.

2. What are the common symptoms of muscular dystrophy?
Common symptoms of muscular dystrophy include muscle weakness, difficulty walking or standing, frequent falls, delayed motor skills development, respiratory difficulties, and in some cases, heart problems. The severity and progression of symptoms can vary depending on the type of muscular dystrophy.

3. How can I support and raise awareness for muscular dystrophy?
There are several ways to support and raise awareness for muscular dystrophy. You can participate in fundraising events, donate to organizations dedicated to research and support, share information and personal stories on social media platforms, and educate others about the disease and its impact.

4. Are there any promising advancements in research and treatment for muscular dystrophy?

Yes, there have been significant advancements in research and treatment for muscular dystrophy. This includes gene therapy, stem cell transplantation, and innovative approaches to managing symptoms. While a cure has not yet been found, ongoing research holds promise for improved therapies and a better understanding of the disease.

15. Eulogy 12 - Farewell, Dear Friend and Colleague: Paying Tribute to a Resilient Co-worker Battling Diabetes

15.1 Introduction: Remembering a Resilient Co-worker and Friend

15.1.1 Remembering a Resilient Co-worker and Friend

Ladies and gentlemen, esteemed family members and friends, it is my solemn duty and privilege today to stand before you as we gather to pay tribute to the life and legacy of our dearly departed. I am [Your Name], [Name]'s [Your relationship to the deceased] and I am honored to speak on behalf of the loved ones gathered here today to pay tribute. In this heartfelt tribute, we pay homage to a dear friend and colleague who battled diabetes with unwavering resilience. Diabetes is a complex disease that affects millions worldwide, and through our personal and professional interactions, we had the privilege of witnessing the indomitable spirit of our co-worker as [he/she] faced the challenges posed by this condition head-on. This eulogy aims to shed light on [His/Her] journey, highlight the importance of support in the workplace, share strategies for managing diabetes at work, and ultimately honor the lasting legacy of our beloved colleague. Join us as we remember [His/Her] strength, achievements, and the impact [He/She] had on our lives and the workplace.

Saying goodbye to a dear friend and colleague is never easy, but when that person has battled a chronic illness like diabetes with unwavering resilience, it's especially poignant. Today, as we bid farewell to our co-worker who has shown incredible strength in the face of adversity, we also want to take a moment to pay tribute to [His/Her] journey and celebrate their resilience.

15.1.2 The Loved Ones who Continue [His/Her] Legacy

Our beloved [Name]'s passing has left a profound void in our lives. In reflecting on [his/her] life, it is important to acknowledge those who continue to carry [his/her] legacy forward. [Name] is survived by [State and name the close kins e.g. [his/her] loving family, including [his/her] devoted [husband/wife] [Name] and their [number] children [List Names], who were the center of [his/her] universe.] [State and name other relatives e.g. [He/She] leaves behind a host of cherished relatives, including nieces, nephews, and cousins whom [he/she] held dear.] Additionally, [he/she] touched the lives of countless friends and acquaintances through [his/her] graciousness and unwavering support. [His/Her] presence will be greatly missed by all who had the privilege of knowing [him/her]. Although this loss brings immeasurable grief, we find solace in knowing that [Name] has engendered a lasting impact on those whose lives [he/she] gracefully enhanced with love and joy.

15.2 Overcoming Challenges: Witnessing Resilience in the Workplace

15.2.1 Balancing Work Responsibilities and Diabetes Management

Managing diabetes entails a multitude of tasks, from monitoring blood sugar levels to administering medication and maintaining a balanced diet. Balancing these responsibilities alongside work commitments can be incredibly challenging. Yet, [Name] has managed to find a way to prioritize [his/her] health while still excelling in their role, showcasing an impressive level of resilience.

15.2.2 Coping with Fluctuating Energy Levels and Health Conditions

Living with diabetes often means dealing with fluctuating energy levels and unpredictable health conditions. Despite this, [Name] has consistently shown up with a positive attitude and a strong work ethic. [He/She] has faced these challenges head-on, reminding us all that resilience is not just about overcoming obstacles but also about embracing them with grace and determination.

15.2.3 Navigating Emotional Well-being and Work Performance

Living with a chronic illness can take a toll on one's emotional well-being, which, in turn, can impact work performance. [Name]'s ability to navigate these emotional ups and downs while maintaining professionalism and productivity has been truly inspiring. [His/Her] resilience serves as a reminder of the importance of mental health support within the workplace.

15.3 Fostering Support and Empathy: The Importance of a Supportive Work Environment

15.3.1 Building a Culture of Understanding and Acceptance

In paying tribute to our co-worker's resilience, we must also acknowledge the role a supportive work environment has played. Fostering a culture of understanding and acceptance is vital for individuals battling chronic illnesses like diabetes. [Name]'s journey reminds us that empathy and compassion are not just buzzwords but essential qualities for creating a workplace where everyone can thrive.

15.3.2 Educating Colleagues about Diabetes and Reducing Stigma

Education is key to breaking down the barriers of stigma and misunderstanding surrounding diabetes. By taking the time to educate ourselves and our colleagues about the disease, we can create a more inclusive environment where individuals with diabetes feel supported and understood. [Name]'s resilience has shown us the transformative power of knowledge and empathy.

15.3.3 Implementing Workplace Accommodations and Support Systems

Providing accommodations and support systems within the workplace is crucial in enabling individuals with chronic illnesses to thrive. From flexible scheduling to access to healthy food options and designated rest areas, these accommodations can significantly ease the burden of managing a condition like diabetes. [Name]'s journey motivates us to advocate for such accommodations and support systems to ensure the well-being of all employees.

As we bid farewell to our remarkable co-worker, we celebrate not only [his/her] professional accomplishments but also [his/her] unwavering resilience in the face of diabetes. [Name]'s journey has taught us the importance of empathy, support, and understanding within the workplace. May we carry [his/her] spirit of resilience with us as we continue to support and uplift each other in our future endeavors. Farewell, dear friend and colleague.

15.4 Celebrating Achievements: Recognizing the Triumphs of a Resilient Co-worker

15.4.1 Highlighting Personal Milestones and Accomplishments

Tip: Living with diabetes requires resilience, determination, and a whole lot of strength. Take the time to celebrate the personal milestones and accomplishments of your co-worker. Whether it's reaching a specific blood sugar target, successfully managing their diabetes during a high-stress project, or making positive lifestyle changes, these achievements deserve recognition.

[**Prompt:** Show your support and appreciation by acknowledging their efforts and sharing their success stories with others. Share stories and memories that highlight their dedication, resilience, and ability to overcome challenges.]

15.4.2 Acknowledging Professional Contributions and Growth

Tip: Beyond their battle with diabetes, your co-worker has likely made significant contributions to the workplace.

[**Prompt:** Take a moment to acknowledge their professional growth and the positive impact they have had on the team. Highlight their accomplishments, whether it's exceeding project goals, mentoring colleagues, or consistently bringing new ideas to the table. By recognizing their professional achievements, you not only honor their contributions but also boost their morale and leave a lasting impression.]

15.5 A - Conclusion: Reflecting on the Impact of a Resilient Co-worker's Battle with Diabetes

In bidding farewell to a dear friend and colleague, it's crucial to reflect on the impact of [his/her] battle with diabetes. [Name] has shown us what it means to face adversity head-on, demonstrating resilience and determination in the face of challenges. Let [his/her] journey inspire us to support one another, prioritize health and wellness, and celebrate the triumphs, both big and small. As we say our goodbyes, may [his/her] departure be a reminder of the strength we all possess and the importance of empathy and understanding in the workplace.

15.5 B - Conclusion: Reflecting on the Impact of a Resilient Co-worker's Battle with Diabetes

As we conclude this tribute, we are reminded of the incredible strength and determination displayed by our resilient co-worker, [Name], in [his/her] battle with diabetes. [Name]'s journey serves as a powerful reminder of the importance of support and understanding in the workplace, not only for individuals living with diabetes but for anyone facing health challenges. Let us carry forward [his/her] legacy by fostering a culture of empathy, advocating for workplace accommodations, and celebrating the triumphs of our colleagues. Farewell, dear friend and colleague - your resilience will forever inspire us.

Diabetes FAQ

1. What is diabetes and how does it impact individuals?

Diabetes is a chronic condition characterized by high blood sugar levels. There are different types of diabetes, including type 1 and type 2. It can have various impacts on individuals, including physical symptoms, the need for medication or insulin management, and potential complications affecting different organs of the body.

2. How can employers create a supportive work environment for employees with diabetes?

Employers can create a supportive work environment by fostering understanding and empathy among colleagues, providing education about diabetes to reduce stigma, offering workplace accommodations such as flexible schedules or designated break times for diabetes management, and implementing wellness programs that promote a healthy lifestyle for all employees.

3. What are some strategies for managing diabetes at work?

Strategies for managing diabetes at work include creating a diabetes management plan in consultation with healthcare professionals, balancing work responsibilities with self-care activities, incorporating physical activity and healthy eating habits into the work routine, and utilizing tools such as glucose monitoring devices or medication reminders to maintain optimal blood sugar levels.

4. How can the achievements and contributions of a co-worker with diabetes be celebrated?

The achievements and contributions of a co-worker with diabetes can be celebrated by acknowledging their personal milestones and professional growth, highlighting their positive impact on the work environment, organizing recognition initiatives such as awards or certificates of appreciation, and establishing a lasting memorial or contribution in their honor.

16. Farewell to Courageous Souls

Writing a eulogy for those we lost to long term illness is a difficult task, as it requires a delicate balance of emotions and reflections. As we pay tribute to the courageous souls who fought bravely against their illnesses. Their journey was one marked by pain and suffering, yet it was also filled with moments of strength and resilience. Now, as we bid them farewell, we must find solace in the knowledge that they are finally free from their physical burdens.

It is with heavy hearts that we say our final goodbye to these remarkable individuals. Each of them faced their long term illnesses with grace and courage, showing us the true meaning of fortitude. Their determination to live their lives to the fullest, despite the challenges that they encountered, is nothing short of inspiring. We will forever cherish the memories we shared, the laughs we had, and the lessons we learned from them.

Though their physical presence may be gone, their spirit lives on within us. We must remember to honor their memory by living our lives with the same bravery and resolve they demonstrated. They teach us the value of appreciating each day and cherishing the time we have with our loved ones. Their endurance serves as a reminder that even in the face of adversity, we have the strength to carry on.

Now, let us find comfort in the knowledge that their suffering has come to an end. As they depart from this world, they leave behind a legacy of strength and resilience that will forever inspire us. We must cherish the memories we have of them and hold them close to our hearts. May we find solace in the belief that they are finally at peace, reunited with those who went before them.

Saying goodbye to those we lost to long term illness is a painful process, filled with sorrow and grief. However, we must also remember the valuable lessons they left behind. Their enduring spirit and unwavering strength serve as a powerful reminder of the human capacity for resilience. As we say our final farewells, let us honor their memory by embracing the preciousness of life and living every moment to its fullest. Though they may be physically gone, their spirits live on within us, forever guiding and inspiring us.

Frequently Asked Questions

A. Writing the Eulogy

A.1 Can anyone contribute to the eulogy for [Name]?

Yes, absolutely. The eulogy is an opportunity for friends, family members, and loved ones to share their personal memories and reflections on [Name]'s life. If you would like to contribute to the eulogy, reach out to the person organizing the service or the individual designated to speak during the ceremony.

A.2 How long should the eulogy be?

The length of the eulogy can vary depending on the traditions, preferences, and time constraints of the memorial service. Generally, a eulogy is around 5 to 10 minutes long, allowing enough time to capture the essence of [Name]'s life and impact. However, it is important to remember that quality matters more than quantity. Focus on sharing meaningful stories and heartfelt messages that truly honor [Name].

A.3 Can I include humor in the eulogy?

Yes, incorporating lighthearted and humorous anecdotes can be a beautiful way to celebrate the joyful moments and unique personality of [Name]. However, it is essential to strike a balance and be mindful of the overall tone of the service. Ensure that any humor is respectful and appropriate for the occasion, keeping in mind the feelings of the grieving family and attendees.

A.4 Is it necessary to follow a particular structure for the eulogy?

While there is no one-size-fits-all structure for a eulogy, it is helpful to have a loose outline to guide your speech. Consider including sections such as an introduction, sharing personal memories, highlighting achievements and contributions, discussing the impact on family and loved ones, and concluding with a heartfelt farewell. However, feel free to adapt the structure to best reflect the unique life and relationship you shared with [Name].

B. The Eulogy and the Healing Process

B.1 Why is delivering a eulogy important in the healing process?

Delivering a eulogy provides an opportunity to express grief, honor the life of the departed, and find solace in shared memories. It allows us to reflect on the impact the person had on our lives and to celebrate their legacy, fostering healing and closure in the grieving process.

B.2 How can I gather memories and stories for a personalized eulogy?

You can gather memories and stories by reaching out to family members, friends, and loved ones who knew the person well. Conduct interviews, ask for personal anecdotes, and encourage others to share their cherished memories. This collaborative approach ensures the eulogy captures the essence of the individual and reflects the collective experiences of those who knew them.

B.3 How do I address the pain and offer comfort in a eulogy?

Addressing the pain and offering comfort in a eulogy can be achieved by acknowledging the difficulties of grief and loss. Share personal reflections on the impact of the sudden illness, express empathy towards others who are mourning, and offer words of comfort, hope, and healing. The eulogy should create a space for collective healing and provide solace to those in attendance.

B.4 What if I find it difficult to write a tribute or express my emotions through words?

Writing a tribute can be challenging, especially when emotions are overwhelming. Take your time and be gentle with yourself. Consider seeking support from others, such as close friends or family members, who can help you brainstorm ideas or even write the tribute together. Alternatively, you can explore other forms of expression like art, music, or creating a visual collage to honor your loved one.

B.5 What role do rituals and symbolism play in a meaningful eulogy?

Rituals and symbolism can add depth and meaning to a eulogy. Consider incorporating rituals, such as lighting candles, sharing symbolic objects, or inviting others to contribute to a memory jar. These gestures can create a sense of sacredness, foster connection, and provide an opportunity for mourners to actively participate in the healing process.

C. Dealing with Memories and Emotions

C.1 How can I cope with the sudden loss of a loved one?

Coping with sudden loss can be an overwhelming and challenging experience. It is important to allow yourself to grieve and feel the full range of emotions. Seek support from friends, family, or a therapist who can provide comfort and guidance during this difficult time. Engaging in self-care activities, such as exercise, journaling, or spending time in nature, can also help in the healing process.

C.2 How can I honor the memory of a loved one who passed away suddenly?

There are various ways to honor the memory of a loved one lost suddenly. You can create a memorial or tribute, such as a photo album, a dedicated webpage, or a charitable foundation in their name. Engaging in activities or causes that were important to your loved one can also serve as a meaningful way to honor their legacy. Additionally, sharing stories and memories with others can help keep their spirit alive.

C.3 Is it normal to feel a mix of emotions, including hope, after experiencing sudden loss?

Absolutely. It is completely normal to experience a wide range of emotions following the sudden loss of a loved one. While grief and sadness may be predominant, it is also possible to feel moments of hope, optimism, and even inspiration. These emotions can stem from the love and connection shared with the departed, as well as from a desire to honor their memory by embracing life and finding meaning in the midst of loss.

C.4 How can sharing memories help in the healing process?

Sharing memories allows us to celebrate the life of our departed loved ones and find comfort in the recollection of cherished moments. It provides an opportunity for reflection, connection, and emotional healing as we share stories, anecdotes, and experiences that keep their memory alive.

C.5 How can I preserve memories in a meaningful way?

Preserving memories can be achieved through various methods. Some common strategies include writing in journals, creating scrapbooks or photo albums, making digital archives, and recording videos. Choose a method that resonates with you and allows you to capture and cherish the memories in a way that feels most meaningful.

D. Grieving and Moving On

D.1 How can I find solace and joy amidst the sorrow of losing someone to sudden illness?

Finding solace and joy amidst sorrow is a personal journey, but there are several strategies that may help. Embracing joyful remembrance by focusing on happy memories and cherished moments can bring comfort. Engaging in activities that celebrate their life, such as creating personalized tributes or participating in rituals of remembrance, can also help in finding solace and healing.

D.2 Is it normal to feel a mix of emotions when grieving the loss of someone to sudden illness?

Absolutely. Grief is a complex and individual experience. It is entirely normal to feel a wide range of emotions, including sadness, anger, guilt, or even moments of joy when reminiscing about the person's life. It is important to give yourself permission to feel and process these emotions in your own time and in your own way.

D.3 How can I navigate the grieving process with the support of my community?

Seeking support from your community can be incredibly helpful during the grieving process. Reach out to family, friends, or support groups who can provide a listening ear and understanding. Sharing stories and memories, attending memorial services, or participating in community events can foster a sense of belonging and provide comfort in knowing that you are not alone in your grief.

D.4 How can I keep the memory of my loved one alive while moving forward with my own life?

Keeping the memory of your loved one alive is a personal and ongoing process. Find ways to honor their legacy by engaging in activities or causes that were important to them. Consider creating rituals or traditions that commemorate their life, such as annual memorial gatherings or participating in activities they enjoyed. Additionally, finding ways to incorporate their values and teachings into your life can keep their spirit alive while also allowing you to move forward and find hope.

D.5 How can memories help in the grieving process?

Memories play a crucial role in the grieving process by allowing us to connect with the essence of our loved ones. They serve as a source of comfort, healing, and inspiration. Memories provide a way to honor the lives of those we have lost, keeping their spirit alive in our hearts.

D.6 Is it beneficial to share memories with others who have experienced a similar loss?

Absolutely. Sharing memories with others who have gone through a similar loss can create a supportive community, providing empathy, understanding, and validation. It allows for the exchange of stories, experiences, and emotions, providing comfort and a sense of connection in the midst of grief.

D.7 What can I do to support someone who is grieving?

Offering support to someone who is grieving can make a significant difference in their healing process. Be present, listen without judgment, and provide a safe space for them to express their emotions. Offer practical help, such as assisting with funeral arrangements or everyday tasks. Most importantly, respect their unique grieving process and be patient with their journey.

D.8 How can I cope with my own grief while supporting others?

Coping with your own grief while supporting others can be challenging. It is essential to establish healthy boundaries, prioritize self-care, and seek support from friends, family, or professionals. Practice active listening and empathy, but also allow yourself the space to grieve. Remember that supporting others does not mean neglecting your own healing process. Seek a balance between comforting others and taking care of yourself.

www.ingramcontent.com/pod-product-compliance
Lightning Source LLC
Chambersburg PA
CBHW030013290326
41934CB00005B/322